THE ROYAL ROAD TO
STAGE HYPNOTISM

The Royal Road to Stage Hypnotism

Mark Lewis

Mark Lewis
Entertainment
Toronto

Mark Lewis Entertainment, Toronto, Canada
https://marklewisentertainment.com

© 2021 Mark Lewis
All rights reserved.

ISBN 978-0-9867329-4-2

Cover art, layout & design by Ariel Frailich

Contents

Foreword vii

Preface ix

Chapter One: What is Hypnosis? 1

Chapter Two: Nuts And Bolts Of Stage Hypnotism 7

Chapter Three: Introductory Lecture 13

Chapter Four: Waking Suggestion Tests........................ 19

Chapter Five: Waking Suggestion On Stage............... 29

Chapter Six: The Hypnotic Induction.......................... 43

Chapter Seven: On With The Show! 49

Chapter Eight: Odds And Ends 83

Chapter Nine: Hypnosis Audio Transcription.......... 99

Chapter Ten: More Extracts From The Audiotape..... 113

Chapter Eleven: Last Word 117

Foreword

What can be said about the book you have purchased? What can be said about the controversial figure who has written the book? Well in each case the answer is quite a bit. In each case some good, some not as good but all worthwhile.

I shall start with the person. Mark Lewis is a controversial (by choice I hasten to add) figure in the world of performance.

The author has been round the world and has penned several other quite good books. I was fully prepared to not particularly enjoy his memoirs "The Lives of a Showman" and was happily able to admit I was incorrect in that assessment. Like it or not the author has a captivating writing style.

As for the book you have purchased it is going to be well worth the time to read. I am not going to ruin the book but I'm betting there are parts of this some stage hypnotists will just disagree with. Go ahead disagree. But don't stop reading! Move past it. The disagreement you have is *not the relevant* part of the show! The insights contained within are far more valuable than any worry about procedure or terminology. It is those insights that will help you to become a better performer and perhaps by thinking of things in a different way will also help you along a little more than a book that falls in line with your perspective.

Danny Doyle
International stage hypnotist

Preface

This book has been written for those people who want to learn the art of putting on hypnotic demonstrations for public entertainment. Whether you be a hypnotherapist, stage entertainer or public speaker wishing to expand your activities, this book will give you the instruction you need. Professional magicians in particular seem to be drawn to this fascinating way of entertaining people.

I believe there is nothing more hilarious than a good demonstration of stage hypnosis. I would also add that there is nothing more dramatic and mysterious than this type of entertainment. A good hypnotism show has everything; comedy, drama, mystery and excitement. One moment the audience is laughing its collective head off, the next moment everyone sits on the edge of their seats, mouths open at some spine chilling demonstration of the weird potential of the human mind.

A word of warning; I would suggest you have experience of speaking in public before attempting this type of work. If you are an experienced performer, teacher or lecturer you are in with a chance. If you are the sort of person who gets nervous in front of a crowd this book is probably not for you. If you are a hypnotherapist wishing to use your skills in a public setting but you have never appeared before an audience you should perhaps postpone your study of this work until this situation is remedied.

Stage hypnotism is not for the faint of heart; you have to have the nerve of the devil. A brass neck with lots of self-confidence. Oh, you should also be a good talker. A famous stage hypnotist once told me when I first started "Get your patter right!" Patter for those of you unacquainted with the word is the jargon used by stage entertainers for the talk used when performing.

The good news is that it is ten times easier to hypnotize people on stage than it is in an individual one on one situation.

The reasons for this will be explained in the first chapter. Suffice it to say that this fact will enable the aspiring hypnotic entertainer to put on a dazzling show if he or she approaches the subject with determination and persistence.

I wish you luck. Your journey has just begun.

CHAPTER ONE
What is Hypnosis?

The title of this chapter should really be "What is *stage* hypnosis?" Stage hypnosis differs appreciably from the type of hypnotism practiced in the office of a hypnotherapist, psychiatrist, doctor or dentist.

For one thing it's easier. Well, easier in the sense of actually putting people into trance. The process of putting a show together, handling a group of volunteers, learning the patter, mastering the techniques of showmanship and above all, entertaining the audience is more challenging and takes a lot of work. The purpose of this book is to help you learn how to put a show on. Instruction will also be given on the art of inducing hypnosis on stage. This last sentence is the easy bit. The sentence before is the hard part. Presenting a 60 to 90 minute public performance is not an easy undertaking; however, putting people into trance in a group situation is simpler than it would at first appear.

In a one to one individual hypnotic session a hypnotherapist can take his time with the patient. A stage hypnotist has to get results fairly quickly. How does he, in a fairly short space of time, get spectacular results that a therapist can only dream of?

Well, you have to realize that the dynamics of the stage situation are completely different. First of all, only the best subjects are kept on stage. The rest are eliminated with the help of various suggestibility tests. If the subject passes the tests he or she is kept on stage. If he or she fails then dismissal back to the audience is the result.

Another factor is that the stage is an alien environment for most people. When a volunteer comes up he is a little disoriented by the situation. The lights, the curtains, the music and sound effects and the presence of the audience all combine to confuse him and make the hypnotic induction a lot easier.

There is also an unseen pressure on the subject to comply with the suggestions of the hypnotist. This pressure comes from the presence of the audience. There is an unspoken expectation by the spectators that the people on stage will respond in the desired way. The hypnotic subjects feel this expectation and will try to please the audience by entering hypnosis. There is also a desire present to please the hypnotist. They feel the expectation and anticipation of both the hypnotist and the audience and succumb to this pressure. There is a feeling of not wishing to be a "party pooper" and it is much easier to go along with the requirements of the situation rather than strike out on one's own individual pathway.

Of course, the above analysis does not answer the question posed by the title of the chapter. What is hypnosis? And in particular, what is stage hypnosis? Actually, it may surprise and perhaps disappoint you that the answer is that I haven't the slightest idea! I'm the hypnotist and even I don't know what is going on! This confession on my part may perhaps cause you to lose confidence in me and deter you from reading further. All I can say in my defence is that I don't think anybody else knows much about it either!

Of course, there are many theories ranging from dissociation to response expectancy. I won't go into the precise explanations of these theories because I don't want to give my readers a headache. Suffice it to say that many eminent psychologists have discussed it, dissected it, torn it apart, chewed it up, spat it out, put it together again, disagreed with each other and in the end we poor students of the human mind are no wiser that when we started!

My position is that if one set of learned psychologists come up with one theory and another equally learned set of psychologists come up with another diametrically opposed theory, then I'm not going to waste my time trying to figure out who is right. After all, if these educated, clever people with degrees and letters after their names can't figure out what hypnotism is what chance have you and I got?

Actually, having said all that, I do have a theory about it-at least where stage hypnosis is concerned. I confess that I'm not a psychologist but sometimes common sense and street-smart experience count more than countless hours of experimentation in a dusty laboratory.

Here's my theory: I don't believe there is any such thing as hypnosis! Yes, that's right! You read me correctly. Even though I have personally influenced thousands of people to jump up and down and act like lunatics on stage I do not believe I have ever hypnotized anyone!

Now before you throw this book away, let me tell you that I am not the only one that has come up with the theory. A lot of stage hypnotists, hypnotherapists and yes, some of the aforementioned learned psychologists also agree with me. To sum up the theory: all the university and psychology studies have been a waste of time since hypnotism doesn't exist in the first place!

Of course, as you can imagine there are a lot of people that don't agree with me. And they may be right! I am not 100% sure that I am correct. Although I don't really believe in hypnotism, I will admit I have seen some very strange behaviour which has at times tempted me to change my mind.

Broadly speaking, psychologists are divided into two camps where hypnosis is concerned. That is, state theorists and non-state theorists. The state theorists believe there is such a thing as a hypnotic state and the non-state theorists believe there isn't.

The book that probably influenced me to become a non-state theorist is entitled "They Call It Hypnosis" by Robert A Baker published by Prometheus Books. Of course, you could read a different book and become a state theorist if you wish. I don't really mind and neither will the author, of course.

Let me explain what I believe happens on stage. I can't speak for what happens in one to one therapy situations since that is not where my level of expertise lies at the present time. I believe that the people who come up on stage all do what they do for different reasons. One person may be an exhibitionist and love showing off, still another may be desirous of experiencing the hypnotic state for reasons of curiosity, another again may be interested because he or she has a weight problem or wishes to give up smoking and is wondering whether an insight into hypnosis will help, still another is simulating a trance state because he or she wants to please the hypnotist. To go off on a temporary tangent, with regard to this simulation of hypnosis, I treat such volunteers according to their acting ability. If they are good actors and really look as if they are hypnotized I will keep them on stage; if they are bad actors that give the appearance of faking it I will send them back to the audience. With regard to the former, they are what is known in the business as "contract players". This means simply that they are not hypnotized but are willing to play along in an unspoken contract between you and them to put on a good show.

Anyway, my point is that people have all sorts of reasons for doing things on stage. Very often, I believe the subjects con themselves into believing that they are hypnotized. Self delusion, basically. They think they are hypnotized and they consequently act in a manner that they think hypnotized people would be expected to act in. This is helped along by the unfamiliar stage situation and environment. They are in a stage of hypnosis because they believe they are! Of course, all this may be a matter of semantics and this state of self delusion is in and of itself, hypnosis. I was once criticized for this theory. A state theorist said I was being too simplistic. Perhaps so, but often obvious truths tend to be quite simple. Intellectuals sometimes can't see the wood for the trees.

Anyway, the important thing from an entertainer's point of view is that hypnosis works on stage. People will do strange things for whatever reason. It is not really the concern of the entertainer whether the word "hypnosis" should be in inverted commas or not. I would recommend the student study and read all he can about the subject so he can form his own theories but in the end, for practical purposes it doesn't really matter a whole lot. The key thing is to put on a good show.

Before I leave this topic I'd like to tell you a story. When I first started my performing career I asked a legendary stage hypnotist for advice. This fellow had retired from the stage and had become a hypnotherapist.

I looked him straight in the eye and asked him straight out, "Are the people on stage really hypnotized? Are they really in some sort of altered state of consciousness or are they just kidding me and themselves?" My guru started to look uncomfortable and become evasive in his answers. However, I persisted and he gave in. He looked shiftily at his receptionist outside in the hallway then closed the door so she wouldn't hear the conversation. He then looked at me and proceeded in a few sentences to explain the key to stage hypnotism. And it was probably the most profound lesson I had ever heard or will hear on the subject. This is what he said. "Look, I was a pioneer in this field. I was number one for about 30 years. In those 30 years I am quite sure I never hypnotized a single person on stage!"

This was quite a shock to me and although I had pushed for the answer, I was nevertheless stunned to receive it. One of the most legendary stage hypnotists of all time had just, in so many words, told me he had been faking it for 30 years! After I recovered I asked him, "Well, in that case, how do you make the people do all those crazy things?" He stared at me and then uttered the key revelation which opened up a new career for me. "You manipulate them, don't you?" You do, of course "manipulate them" and I've been manipulating them ever since.

CHAPTER TWO
Nuts And Bolts Of Stage Hypnotism

Now how do you put on a good show? And how on earth do you rehearse it? Well, the rest of this book will tell you how to put on the show. This chapter will tell you how to rehearse it.

Rehearsing a hypnotism show is a tricky prospect. Unlike an actor rehearsing his lines for a play or a public speaker learning his script the operation of a hypnosis show is not entirely under the operator's control. You have the volunteer subjects to worry about. Some of them will react well; some may not react at all. This is why every hypnosis show is different. Even though the same programme and routines are presented on separate occasions the show itself becomes entirely different because of the unpredictability of the volunteers. At one show a routine may get a mild reaction, at another the same routine may bring the house down simply because you have a different subject taking part.

So, how can you rehearse and practice a thing like this? And where do you get the experience in trance induction if you have never hypnotized anyone in your life?

To answer both questions I'm going to backtrack a little and tell you that the standard wisdom for stage hypnotism neophytes is that they should have had lots of prior experience hypnotizing people in a one to one situation before setting foot on a public stage. This is ideal if you happen to be a hypnotherapist wishing to perform in public. Unfortunately, if you do not happen to be a hypnotherapist this advice, in my opinion, could actually slow your progress.

When I first started, I tried to follow this wisdom but I found it hard to secure eager guinea pigs to experiment with. And when I did find someone brave enough to help me, I did not find they would go under hypnosis anyway. By the way, it is much easier to hypnotize strangers than it is to induce a trance (a hypnotic one, anyway) among your friends and relatives.

This is because people who know you well will not have the confidence in your ability that is so important in the operator-subject relationship.

The other standard wisdom for budding performers is that they should study as much about hypnosis as possible before starting. Apparently, you should absorb and learn as much as you can about trance induction, dissociation, trance logic and confabulation, etc.

Quite frankly, and with all due deference to the authorities who give the above instruction, you don't have the time. You are going to have enough trouble learning how to put on an entertaining show without the added strain of absorbing lots of impractical material.

My advice, therefore, is to forget all the theory and get straight to the meat of the thing. Ignore the fluff, get up on that stage and entertain people. I am not saying disregard hypnotic theory entirely. In fact, the more the merrier. But not at the expense of learning how to be a showman on stage. Study the stuff, certainly; but it should be an ongoing study rather than a preliminary requirement.

Of course, I'm a little biased in view of my previously stated opinion that the hypnotic state doesn't exist anyway! I suppose I'm basically saying why study something that doesn't exist in the first place? However, I'm not saying don't learn anything at all. I'm saying you should learn to *manipulate* the people and if you want to call this manipulation "hypnotism" that's fine by me. Only, do this on *stage* and not in the recesses of your mind. Basically, I'm suggesting you get on with the job.

As mentioned, the accepted rule is that the budding stage hypnotist should have had acquired hypnotic experience before performing in public. Actually, I believe the rule should be reversed. It is my contention that the potential performer should have had lots of experience appearing in public before demonstrating hypnosis on stage. This is because the actual trance induction in a public situation is relatively easy to do;

the hard part is making a show out of it. This is where a seasoned entertainer or public speaker comes into his own.

Before I leave the subject, I will tell you another story to illustrate my possible controversial theory that you don't have to know that much about hypnotism before performing on stage. I read this years ago and it amused and educated me at the time.

Once upon a time, a cowboy singer and a stage hypnotist were touring across America. The cowboy would open the show by doing his rope spinning and western songs after which the mesmerist would perform his spellbinding show. There was a certain amount of friction between the two entertainers mainly on account of the cowboy's drinking habits. He would often perform in a state of intoxication that offended the hypnotist's sense of professionalism. One night, matters came to a head when the cowboy showed up for the performance even more inebriated than usual. The hypnotist was furious and refused to perform on the same stage as our alcoholic friend, whereupon the cowboy slurred, "Who cares if you don't go on; I can do your act just as well as my own!" So saying, he staggered out on stage and recited the hypnotist's patter word for word just as he had heard it every night for the preceding three months. He performed the hypnotist's exact act and created a sensation. All the subjects went into trance and performed in the usual way despite the cowboy's intoxication and lack of experience. After this incident, the cowboy and the hypnotist, not surprisingly, parted company. The sequel to the tale is that the cowboy turned hypnotist subsequently went on to become one of the most famous stage hypnotists of his generation.

The moral of the anecdote is that you don't have to be a hypnotist to perform stage hypnotism, but you do have to be an entertainer. If you doubt this statement, think of all the stage hypnotists who have become hypnotherapists (rather a lot) and compare this to the amount of hypnotherapists who have become entertainers (not so many). It works one way and not the other. You have to have experience on stage but you don't have to know too much about hypnosis. I rest my case.

Of course, I still haven't told you how to rehearse, have I? Patience, dear reader, I'm coming to it now. The purpose of the above rambling was to tell you that you don't really have to study anything before you start; just get straight to the rehearsal. As already mentioned, you should be used to appearing in public, but that's about it as far as preparation goes.

With regard to the aforementioned unpredictable results of hypnosis the approach I suggest will take a bit of nerve. However, a good stage hypnotist needs a lot of audacity, brazenness and self-confidence.

I believe your best mode of operation is to study the routine in this book, or failing that, any routine that particularly appeals to you and rehearse it out loud to the tables and chairs at home! Simply imagine that you have volunteers on stage and they are doing everything exactly as you require. Just assume your invisible helpers are cooperating with all your suggestions. This way you will be performing a spellbinding and funny show in your own mind, at least.

Thoroughly learn the act making particularly sure that you "get your patter right" as mentioned in the introduction to this book. I am going to repeat that. "GET YOUR PATTER RIGHT". I believe this is the whole key to performing a hypnotism show for the first time. By thoroughly knowing what you are going to say before you say it, you will avoid nervousness and exhibit the self-confidence that is utterly necessary in this type of work. Rehearse, rehearse and rehearse again. And keep on rehearsing until you are sick of it. If your time is limited and you don't want the thing to degenerate into drudgery you could keep to a plan of practicing at least one hour a day for, say, three months. This rehearsal can get a little tedious but the results will pay off a thousand-fold in the long run. When you hear the audience laugh, when you sense your spectators are spellbound, when you hear after-the-show compliments, and above all when you count the money earned from your performances you will know all the hard work will have been worth it.

However, you do have to be determined and persistent. You also have to be brave. The determination and persistence will be necessary at the rehearsal; the bravery will be needed when you do your first show before an audience. If your first show fails you will have to be extra brave for your second show. And determined. And persistent. Keep at it; you'll get there in the end.

I was lucky. My first public show was quite a success. Unfortunately, my subsequent seven or eight shows were, shall we say, a little on the mediocre side. If I hadn't had success on my first show I'm not sure if I would have persisted.

This is where you have to be brave, determined and persistent. If you get good results when you first start performing, well, congratulations. Your practice and rehearsal have paid off. If you continue to get results on a consistent basis, even more congratulations are in order. However, if you do not get good results straight away, or even for a while, you still deserve congratulations for persisting.

If things go well, so much the better for you, if things go badly so much the worse for you. Whatever happens, good or bad you must *persist*. If you do, you will get there in the end.

CHAPTER THREE
Introductory Lecture

Most stage hypnotists commence their show with an introductory lecture. The purpose of this is twofold. First, it helps to establish your personality to the audience. If as a result of the opening speech the audience takes to you personally, it will be that much easier to attract enthusiastic volunteers. If people like you they will be more inclined to come up on stage. You have won their confidence and they will trust you not to mistreat them. Furthermore, if the audience approves of your personality they are more likely to approve of the show. Actually, if they approve of the show it will be much easier to put the volunteers under hypnosis. This is because, if you have suggestible subjects, they will sense the approval of the audience and go into trance more readily. Conversely, this volunteer suggestibility will work against you if they pick up on the fact that the audience does not like the personality of the performer and as a result is lukewarm about the show. The volunteers may resist hypnosis because they sense the crowd is antagonistic. It therefore behooves you to be as pleasant as possible during your introduction so as to get on the good side of the group. Smile, look at people, be agreeable and friendly during your opening remarks and you will set the stage for an entertaining show.

The second purpose of your introduction is to impress the audience with your credentials. You must convey the impression that you are an absolute expert on the subject of hypnosis. It must seem that you have studied the subject for many years and you should imply by your words and manner that you have hypnotized thousands of people. If you are inexperienced in hypnosis, do not let it show. I repeat, *the audience must think you are an expert.* If they suspect that you are a beginner they will not go into trance. Even if it is your first performance and you have never hypnotized anyone in your life don't let it show. Be calm and talk with apparent authority. Use big words if you like; if you use a few technical terms here and there it will tend to convince the audience that you know what you are talking about. Even if you don't! This is where nerve comes in. I mentioned on previous pages the necessity of a brass neck and the nerve of the devil. Now you see why! It may seem somewhat cynical for me to say so but I believe the purpose of your introduction is to "con" the audience into believing you are an authority on hypnosis. Actually, in time you will be, with experience. Of course, you have to bear in mind my cynical point of view, already expressed, that hypnotism doesn't exist anyway! I suppose I am saying you should imply expertise in a subject that is probably illusionary in nature.

Anyhow, you talk for a few minutes before starting the main body of the show. What you say is of course up to you. I will give two typical examples of opening speeches but you don't have to stick to them slavishly. Alter them around a little bit to reflect your own personality. By all means make up your own little spiel if you like. The only advice I would give you is to make it sound slightly scientific and not too long. By all means, study other stage hypnotists and see what they say in their opening remarks or even better, get other books on stage hypnosis and see what examples you can find of introductory lectures which you feel would suit you. Anyway, here's a couple to get you started.

Introductory Lecture 1

"Tonight I want to demonstrate to you the power of hypnosis. Now, what is hypnosis? Is it something dark, strange and mysterious? No. It's simply the power of suggestion. Relaxation of the mind, relaxation of the muscles. Now, you know, many people find it difficult to relax their muscles. When a doctor examines your throat he'll often use an instrument to push your tongue down. That's because you find it difficult to relax the muscles of your tongue.

When we sleep our muscles are completely relaxed. The idea is to emulate this state in the daytime when we are awake. You know, thousands of people suffer nervous difficulties; they feel tired and irritable because their muscles and nerves are under continual tension. The person that can learn to relax their muscles is the person who adds zest to their life."

At this point I normally demonstrate the hand relaxation test described in the next chapter but if you prefer you can continue thus:

"Now, I believe hypnosis is a state of relaxed suggestibility. I've talked to you about relaxation. What about suggestion? Well, suggestion has been defined as the subconscious realisation of an idea. In other words, an idea bypasses the critical judgement of the conscious mind and manifests itself in the more accepting realm of the subconscious. Let me illustrate this idea with a little experiment in the power of suggestion."

At this point you can perform one of the waking suggestion tests described in the next chapter. The lemon test would be a particularly good one to use at this point.

Introductory Lecture 2

"Ladies and gentlemen, in a few moments I am going to invite a committee of volunteers to occupy these chairs and experience the phenomena of hypnosis. Before doing so, however, I think a few words of explanation about hypnotism would not go amiss. What is hypnotism? Well, according to university studies it has been defined as an extension of concentration. The best hypnotic subjects are the ones who can focus well and concentrate strongly. I must tell you that hypnotism is no longer used solely for entertainment. It has been recognized by the British and American medical associations as having great therapeutic value. If you can learn to enter hypnosis you can help yourself to lose weight, stop smoking, cure phobias and improve study habits. Hypnosis has been used to alleviate chronic pain and in fact was used in early operations before anaesthetics were discovered. Psychologists and psychiatrists have used hypnosis effectively in their practices and by and large, I believe hypnosis has great benefit for mankind. Hypnotism is based on the power of suggestion. Tonight I would like to illustrate this power with a little experiment."

Now you follow with a waking suggestion test as described in the next chapter.

Somewhere in your introductory remarks it would be a good idea to give a little warning such as the following:

"In a few moments, I am going to invite some volunteers up on stage to take part in the hypnotic experience. Now, what I do is safe, fun and entertaining. The people that come up here will have a better time than the people in the audience. But please use common sense when you volunteer. For example, if you suffer from epilepsy or heart trouble you really don't want to be up here. Not because hypnosis brings on an attack but if an attack happens the hypnotist gets blamed for it and I don't want to get blamed for it. Furthermore, I would discourage expectant mothers or people who are physically disabled from volunteering. Now, here's an important one. If you suffer from any psychiatric disturbance hypnotism can sometimes be a wonderful therapy but not tonight, not up here and not by me. You do require a good psychologist, doctor or psychiatrist-not an entertainer. However, if you are in reasonable physical and mental health I will be delighted to have you join me on stage."

The above remarks will help to protect you from unsuitable subjects who could give you trouble or even sue you for alleged physical or mental harm caused by the show. I will go into this matter in more detail later on but for now suffice it to say that a warning such as the above could save you quite a bit of trouble. Even with this protection, however, a few unsuitable people, particularly the mentally disturbed could find their way on stage but at least you have covered yourself to a significant degree by using the above wording. It makes you appear responsible and in the unlikely event of trouble occurring you can at least argue that you gave fair warning. It behooves you, of course, to observe your volunteers carefully and if you have any doubts about the physical or mental health of anyone, to send that person back to their seat in the audience.

It is also advisable to inform the audience that you cannot allow anyone under the age of 16 to come on stage. It is asking for trouble for very young people to come up on stage to be put under hypnosis without the consent of their parents (or even WITH their consent!). In fact there are even laws in certain jurisdictions forbidding this.

After you have established your personality with the introductory lecture you now proceed with various waking suggestion tests. These will be explained fully in the next chapter.

CHAPTER FOUR
Waking Suggestion Tests

You are now at a point where you are ready to demonstrate what is known as waking suggestion. I usually start with the following test. It arouses interest and gives the audience a chance to participate.

The Hand Relaxation Test

I usually say something like this, "It's harder to relax your muscles than you might at first suppose. If I place a book, a heavy book on the palm of my hand and remove my hand quickly it is obvious that the book will fall to the floor. There can be no question about it. It's the law of gravity. In the same way, if I place my left hand on the forefinger of my right hand and remove my finger speedily it is obvious that the hand will fall. However, if the left hand and arm are not completely relaxed, if you don't put yourself in a passive, relaxed state, when you remove the finger the arm will not fall. It will remain where it is. Static."

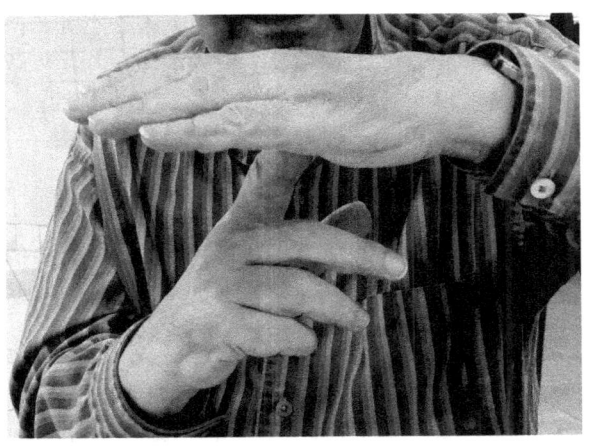

Demonstrate all this with your own hands as you speak. Continue, "Let's try a little experiment here. Let's find out how relaxed you really all are. Everybody place their left hand onto the right forefinger just like this" Demonstrate as you talk, placing your own left hand onto your right forefinger as in the photograph.

"Now are you sure you are all doing that correctly? Let the full weight rest on the finger. Now on the count of three remove the finger and the hand will drop like a dead weight. Ready? One, two, three!"

Remove your finger and drop your left hand. Observe the audience. Many of the hands will have dropped into the lap but many others will still remain static and stuck in the air.

You now continue, "Ah, I see that some of you are able to relax, yet some of you will have to concentrate more so we'll try it again. Come on everybody; left hand on the right forefinger. That's it. Now on the count of three remove the finger and the arm and hand will fall. One two three!"

You repeat the test here but you will find that on this second occasion you will get more people dropping their hands thus revealing to you that they are more likely to follow instructions and enter hypnosis.

Continue, "Ah, you are getting in to the swing of it now. I believe hypnosis is a state of relaxed suggestibility. We have talked about relaxation. What about suggestibility?"

You can now continue with:

The Lemon Test

The lecture continues: "Well, let me suggest to you the idea of a lemon. An invisible lemon." Hold your left hand as if you are in possession of a lemon. Stare at it as if it is real. "This lemon is so sour and so bitter. I am now going to cut it in half with an invisible knife." Mimic the actions of cutting with the unoccupied right hand. "And as I cut it in half the juice is dripping to the floor. My hand is all sticky with the juice. Sticky with the juice. Because that lemon is so sour and so bitter. And now I am going to taste that sour, bitter lemon. Oh it is sour! It is bitter! And as I taste it you can actually taste it too. Your mouths are filling up with saliva as you taste that sour bitter lemon. Really, really sour" As you recite the foregoing you bring the "lemon" up to your mouth as if you are actually tasting it. Grimace as you taste it. This will help the power of suggestion to take effect.

You now ask the audience, "O.K. Now hands up those of you who could actually taste that lemon to some degree? Who actually experienced the sour taste?" Some hands will always go up. You respond, "You see. That is an example of the power of suggestion at work. There is no actual lemon here. It is simply what is called the subconscious realization of an idea. The idea of a lemon is placed in your deeper mind. The salivary glands secrete and you actually experience the taste of a lemon. Of such is the power of suggestion."

Now you can go on to:

The Itching Test

Continue, "Here is another example. I call it the itching test. You see the mind affects the skin. When we are embarrassed we blush, when we are afraid we go white, and when we are angry the skin goes livid. And when I say the word "itch" you feel like you want to scratch, don't you? Even the very word makes you itch. Well, I will say the word slowly and you will feel the effect more. I-t-c-h. I-t-c-h. I-t-c-h! (draw the word out slowly) Now if you want to scratch, go ahead. Your arms are itchy, your legs are itchy, between your shoulder blades at the back. And there is one place on your body itching more than anywhere else. Scratch that itch away! Your skin is itching and irritated, itching and irritated, itch, itch, itch, scratch that itch away!"

As you continue in this vein you will actually see members of the audience scratching themselves. What you are doing here with this little test is developing rapport with the crowd and establishing your credibility. This will make it easier to hypnotize your volunteers when the time comes.

Now you banish the itchy sensation thus, "All right now everybody, you are in a pool of water, cool pleasant calming water, your skin feels smooth and pleasant, smooth and pleasant and all the itching has gone away. Just relax and everything is fine."

Everybody will now stop scratching. Continue, "Hands up those of you that could feel that itching effect to some degree" The hands in the audience will go up. You say, "That is another example of the power of suggestion at work. Now in a few moments I am going to ask for some volunteers to come up here and take part in the hypnotic experience."

At this point I insert the remarks I explained earlier about warning the audience not to volunteer if they suffer from epilepsy, heart trouble etc. You can now invite your volunteers up. I prefer however to do a couple more suggestibility tests since they are good entertainment in themselves. This next one is my favourite.

Magnetic Fingers

Continue, "Let's try another experiment. Everybody, interlock your fingers as if in prayer." Illustrate with your own hands assuming a "prayer" position. See photograph.

"Now extend your two index fingers straight out like this." Illustrate with your own fingers holding them extended about an inch apart from each other. Continue, "That's it, about an inch apart from each other. Now stare at the tips of those fingers. Concentrate on your own fingers. Do not look at your neighbor. Imagine in your mind that there are tiny magnets at the tips of your fingers. Those magnets are so strong, so very strong that they are beginning to pull your fingers together. They are moving in, closing in, getting nearer and nearer, you cannot resist the influence" The fingers will indeed move in towards each other not because of the power of suggestion but because of physiological reasons. It is quite a strain NOT to stop them

moving in toward each other! The fingers are in an uncomfortable position and will tend to move in anyway. The audience members that try this will sometimes become quite alarmed at what is happening and you will hear gasps all over the audience as you direct this little stunt. This will reinforce the audience belief in your ability and your prestige will be enhanced. The higher your prestige the easier it will be to hypnotize people.

To go off on a temporary tangent this business of building prestige is very important. As already stated, you must appear to be an EXPERT. Anything you can do to build this prestige from the way you dress and the way you present yourself even offstage will be very useful when you actually induce "trance" in the volunteers. I am putting the word "trance" in inverted commas since, as already explained I am not sure if there is such a thing anyway.

With regard to the prestige thing, the fact that you are on stage in the first place gives you prestige. Any advance publicity such as posters etc; will help you in this regard. I cannot emphasize enough how important this factor of prestige is.

Anyway, back to the magnetic fingers stunt. After a while you will see people's fingers actually touching together. Continue, "And now your fingers are beginning to touch together, slowly coming together until they touch. And now they are touching. And as they touch you find that they are actually beginning to stick together. They are sticking so tightly together that they are stuck! Stuck tight, tight together and you cannot separate them no matter how hard you try. Try, try hard! You cannot separate them no matter how hard you try. The more you try the more you find that they are stuck. Stuck tight, tight together. Glued, stuck and bonded"

Quite a bit of consternation will ensue as people will try and separate their fingers! A kind of mass hysteria sets in which makes it quite hard, believe it or not, for people to do such a simple thing as separate the two index fingers which seem to all intents and purposes to be permanently stuck to each other.

When you feel you have had enough fun out of the situation you say, "All right now. The magnetic influence will be gone on the count of three. One, two three! You can relax and the fingers will come apart." And they do. Actually, sometimes they don't! You will occasionally come across a very few suggestible people that get in such a state of excitement that even after you give the separation suggestion they are still struggling to get the two fingers apart. This will add to the merriment of the audience if you point them out. Sometimes, I go into the audience and help them to separate the fingers. I tell them to relax completely and try to separate their interlocked fingers one at a time. Part of the reason the index fingers are still stuck is that the hands are still locked in the "prayer" position and the excitement of the moment has caused the subject to lock the hands so tightly that some kind of mild mental paralysis sets in and they can't gather their thoughts to figure out how to do a simple thing like separate the hands!

Anyway, I usually tell them to relax each finger one at a time. I touch each finger and help them to do this. Eventually they manage, they separate the fingers and I direct the audience to give them a big round of applause.

Time for another tangent. This business of directing the applause to the participants rather than taking the glory yourself is very important for a stage hypnotist. It is good practice to do this at the end of some particularly effective routine or skit. You are not the star of the show –they are. Stars of the show like applause. If they get it they perform better. It is a similar thing with your volunteers. If they feel that the audience appreciates what they do then they will do it better. They will respond by becoming more animated and be more prone to the suggestions that are made. They will also realize that they are doing the right thing. If the audience is silent then the participants have no idea if they are doing what they are supposed to be doing. Conversely the more enthusiastic the audience reaction the stronger will be the volunteer reaction. In fact I use this in my patter. I often say "Ladies and gentlemen, the stronger the audience response the stronger will be the hypnotic response so please give our volunteers a fantastic round of applause!"

It also makes the subjects feel that what they are doing is important. If they feel that they are doing something worthwhile they will react accordingly. Conversely, if they feel that the audience is not responsive they will be discouraged from being responsive themselves. I touched on this at the beginning of Chapter Three.

But back to business. You now follow with a great suggestibility test. This is a very popular stunt that is used by many stage hypnotists the world over.

Handlocking Test

This works on physiological principles just as the preceding "magnetic fingers" test does.

Ask the entire audience to raise their hands in the air. Tell them to interlock their fingers and turn their hands inwards and outwards with the palms facing the ceiling. Demonstrate with your own hands as you do this.

Say, "As you push your hands up towards the ceiling you are beginning to feel that your arms are becoming stiff and rigid.

Like poles of iron. And you find that your fingers are bulging and swelling. Bulging and swelling. And your hands are beginning to stick tight, tight together. In fact they stick so tightly together that you cannot separate them. Try. Try hard to separate them. You find that you cannot. You cannot separate them. Because they are stuck, tight, tight, tight together. They are glued together, bonded together, stuck together and you cannot separate them no matter how hard you try."

The audience will now be in a state of excitement because they find that their hands are indeed stuck together. Some will be able to separate them but many won't. Your repeated suggestions will confuse them further and they will not be able to figure out how to bring the hands apart. Of course, it is a very awkward thing physically to unclasp the hands when they are in this unnatural position anyway but you don't tell the audience that. All is fair in love and entertainment. You want to put on a good show and a little subterfuge goes a long way in achieving this.

Many hypnotists now ask the people with their hands locked to come up on stage saying, "If you come on stage I will personally separate your hands for you." This way they get their volunteers to take part in the show.

I prefer to release everybody from their predicament by saying, "All right. I am taking away the magnetic influence on the count of three. One, two, three, relax-it's all gone. All gone. You can now separate your fingers. Everything is fine."

Once the audience has gathered its collective thoughts together everyone will figure out how to separate the hands. Of course just as in the previous "magnetic fingers" test a few people will still be stuck. I make a big deal out of this and will often bring one of the "stuck" people on stage. This of course will disorient them even more and make it even harder for them to unlock the hands. I make a big show of getting them to relax finger by finger so that they can release the hands.

They get a big round of applause and they go back to the audience.

Now it is time to invite your volunteers on stage and do a few further tests on them. I will explain all this in the next chapter.

CHAPTER FIVE
Waking Suggestion On Stage

In this chapter I will describe the invitation of spectators to come on stage and further waking suggestion tests that you do on these people.

I usually say, "Without further ado may I ask anyone that wishes to volunteer to come right on up and fill up the chairs which you see in front of you."

This would be a good point to explain the chair set up. The amount of chairs you use will depend a lot on the venue and the circumstances. I have used as many as 20 chairs and as little as 6. If you have a large audience and a large stage you will use more chairs. If you have either a small audience or only a limited amount of stage space you will only use a few chairs.

When I perform at high schools I will use a large amount of chairs because the audience response at this type of venue is very strong and I often get more people on stage than I can handle. Auditorium stages at high schools tend to be quite large so there is plenty of room to fit all the eager beavers that want to volunteer.

Actually, nowadays I use around 12 to 15 chairs on average. I found that in earlier years when I would use more it could get a bit unwieldy to handle all the volunteers. I would say in most cases I use about a dozen depending on the size of the stage or performing area.

This would be a good place to explain that the response of the audience when you ask for volunteers will often be an indication as to how well your show is going to go. If they rush up to the stage with great enthusiasm you are likely to have a great show on your hands. If you get too many people and have to send some back you are probably going to have quite a successful program. If on the other hand they come up in dribs and drabs in a reluctant fashion you are going to have to pull out all the stops in order to get positive results. It can be done but you are going to have to be a real showman with nerves of steel in order to do it. This is where the men will be separated from the boys.

I am going to go off on another tangent now. If you find that volunteers are slow in coming DO NOT PANIC. Just take your time. Relax. If you panic you can ruin the show which may be tough going as it is anyway. If you panic you will end up talking too fast and look amateurish and nervous. Any volunteers you do get will not go into trance because they must have confidence in the hypnotist. If he appears unsettled, they in turn will also become unsettled and the results will not be good.

Slow down and think to yourself, "I am not going to go anywhere. The show can't continue without me. I will take my own sweet time. I will take as long as I need to get a committee. I don't care if it takes me half an hour"

Of course, you will indeed care if it takes half an hour! However, you say this to yourself as a way of calming your mental attitude. Just take your time and say pleasant humorous things such as, "Take your time but hurry up!" Say this with a smile, though. Another one I use is, "You are all very slow. Do you work for the post office?" This will get a laugh and break the ice. Never appear tense. You will make matters worse if you do. Just think that you are going to get the committee no matter how long it takes. You are the master.

I will sometimes say, "Don't all rush at once!" or, "If you move your legs forward you will find that your body will automatically follow!" Just play for time and relax. You will get your volunteers if you wait for them.

On no account should you say things like, "If I don't get volunteers I won't be able to do a show." It will be the kiss of death if you say something like this. Never insult your audience or be aggressive in any way. Look expectant and smile. You can even look at one or two friendly people and ask them directly. I normally like to ask for volunteers rather than pick them out but here we can make an exception.

Waking Suggestion On Stage

In practice you will usually find that if volunteers are a bit slow the person that booked you or people connected with the committee that engaged you will often volunteer because they want a successful show.

To illustrate the importance of not panicking I really must show you a sequence of photographs which will illustrate the point quite splendidly!

These are pictures of a stage hypnotism show at an outdoor event some time ago. To my horror when I stepped out on stage there was nobody in the audience because of the rain. My assistant thought it would be terribly amusing to take secret pictures of the impending catastrophe. After all, how was I supposed to get volunteers when there was nobody in the audience?!! As explained I have learned not to panic so just kept on talking and slowly a crowd gathered bit by bit and in the end I had a very successful show. A friend of mine was very impressed by the pictures and became very philosophical, finding in them a deep meaning about the struggle of life in general. He felt that they sent a message about resilience and not giving in even when the odds are against you. I don't know about all that but I shall certainly be satisfied if the photos illustrate the message never to panic when asking for volunteers and few, if even any, are forthcoming!

At first, nobody shows up...

... then, slowly, a few brave souls venture...

... encouraged, people start entering...

... word spreads and a crowd builds...

Waking Suggestion On Stage

... until, finally, the show can begin!

I have spent more space on this than I intended but it will be useful information for the times that response is sparse when asking for people to come up on stage.

Anyway, your volunteers now trek on to the stage to experience hypnosis. Once they take their seats on stage direct the audience to give them a hearty round of applause. You remark "You see! They love you already and you haven't even done anything yet!" This remark will garner amusement and more importantly help you to gain rapport with the volunteers.

You now check out your volunteers and see what you have. This is your first chance to sum up your participants and judge whether they should be on stage or not. It is too early to decide but you can get an initial impression of their attitude. If someone is aggressive or overly showing off they might be a candidate for removal once you get going. If on the other hand they appear eager and friendly you may have a good subject.

Now at this point the standard wisdom in stage hypnosis circles is to separate friends or couples who come up together. You make people switch seats around. The reason for this is that people who are together may distract each other by having whispered conversations under their breath thus interfering with the smooth running of the show.

I have always believed this myself and up to the time of writing have followed the procedure of separating people who come up together. However, just lately I have been wondering if this is indeed a wise procedure to follow. I am undergoing a sea change in my attitude in regard to this.

I have noticed that people who are separated tend to feel isolated and less inclined to enter hypnosis than if a familiar presence is beside them. I have even seen a look of slight panic when they find their familiar friend or spouse is directed to sit away from them. I am inclined now to think that the person is more liable to enter hypnosis if their companion is beside them.

From this point on I will not be separating couples or people who come up together unless I see that one of the two is particularly talkative on stage.

I apologize to my readers for my change in procedure happening just at the time I write a book on hypnosis. I expect students like their teachers to know what they are doing and not be changing their minds in mid stream. I can only say that I have been concerned with this matter for some time and I think it is now time to change my standard procedure. I would urge my readers to make their own minds up about this and perhaps try it both ways. I do promise my literary audience that from now on in this book there will be no further change of procedures to confuse the student!

At this point I usually make a little speech to the audience. It has several purposes; first it adds a little humor to the proceedings, second it gives me another chance to evaluate my volunteers, third it educates the volunteers and the audience at the same time and fourth it tends to dissuade uncooperative participants.

I say, "There are three types of persons who cannot be hypnotized. First if you are drunk I cannot hypnotize you." Observe the volunteers carefully at this point. Often one or two of them will think they are great humorists and will pretend to leave the stage. After they have made their little joke, they will of course return to their seats. They have, however, given away the fact that they are exhibitionists and will make good subjects for your purposes whether they enter "trance" or not.

I continue, "The second type of person who cannot be hypnotized is someone who is mentally challenged. In other words not too bright." Watch the volunteers here. Again, some bright sparks will pretend to leave the stage. These little antics from the potential subjects will enhance the entertainment value of the show as it gets the audience laughing. However, it serves a deeper purpose by allowing you to evaluate who the good subjects are likely to be. These people who pretend to leave the stage have proved themselves to enjoy a bit of fun and play along with the situation so they should be noted for later on.

I continue on, "The third type of person who cannot be hypnotized is someone who doesn't want to be hypnotized. For example, if you come up here with a challenge and say 'I bet you can't hypnotize me' well guess what? You are correct. I cannot hypnotize anyone that doesn't want to be hypnotized so there is no point in me trying and you would be better off watching the show from the audience"

These last few sentences warn the volunteers that you need their full cooperation and there is no point in them resisting you deliberately.

At this point you are ready to commence what are known as waking suggestion tests. You have of course already done a few of these with the entire audience but this is the first time you will perform them on stage.

Address the group thus: "At this point I want to demonstrate waking suggestion in hypnosis. You will not be put into hypnosis just yet. This is just to see if you would possess the requirements to be good hypnotic subjects"

You continue, "Put your arms straight out in front of you like this. Palms towards the floor" Illustrate what you mean with your own arms stretching them out in front of you with the palms of the hands towards the floor. Continue, "Close your eyes." As an aside to the audience you now say with a smile, "They all look like sleepwalkers, don't they?"

Continue with the test thus:

"Turn your right hand palm up." The volunteers do so. The position now is that everyone has their arms outstretched in front of them and the right hand is palm up towards the ceiling and the left hand is palm down towards the floor.

Continue, "Imagine in your mind that there is a heavy weight, a very heavy weight attached to your right wrist. This weight is so very heavy that it is pulling your right arm down, down towards the floor. Lower and lower towards the floor. At the same time there is a large balloon filled with helium attached to your left wrist pulling your left arm up towards the ceiling. Up, up it goes. Right arm is being pulled down lower and lower and the left arm is being pulled up higher and higher."

Continue the suggestions in this vein and at this point you are watching the volunteers carefully. With some of them the arms will hardly move at all and with others you will see that one arm is being pulled down and the other up. The people that it is working well on will probably be your best subjects and the people who do not respond will in most cases be your worst. However, this is just a guideline and is not cast in tablets of stone since I have had what seem to be non responsive subjects eventually comply and at times the responsive ones do exactly the opposite! Generally, however, the rule holds true that those who cooperate well in the waking suggestion tests will be excellent hypnotic subjects.

Continue: "Your right arm is being pulled down lower and lower. You cannot resist. Down, down it goes. Your left arm is being pulled higher and higher. Up, up it goes.

Right arm down lower and lower. Left arm up higher and higher."

"Now I'm placing a second weight to your right wrist pulling your right arm down twice as much as it is now. Twice as much as it is now. At the same time, I am attaching a second balloon to your left wrist pulling your left arm up twice as much as it is now. Twice as much as it is now. Right arm going down lower and lower, left arm going up higher and higher. You cannot resist the influence."

Keep repeating the suggestions along this line and you will see a few people complying with great responsiveness, a few moderately successful results and a few mediocre duds.

Tell them to freeze in the position they are now in and under no account move from that position. Now instruct them to open their eyes and see how they got on still keeping in position. You will often get a laugh here when the subjects look around and see how their individual responsiveness varies from that of their colleagues on stage. After you have derived sufficient amusement from this you tell your volunteers to relax and put their hands in their laps.

One explanatory note here may be in order. The reason for asking at the beginning of the test for the right arms to be turned up facing the ceiling is a physiological one. The right arm is more liable to drift downwards when you do this since it is slightly uncomfortable to hold the arm in this position. However, it is only fair to point out that not all hypnotists follow this procedure. Many simply ask the volunteers to stretch out both arms with the palms down.

I once asked an experienced stage hypnotist why he didn't follow the procedure of asking the volunteers to turn the right arms palm up because I reasoned that they would respond better that way. He replied, "To do it that way is not a true test of suggestion." He may have a point and possibly he thought that when he later selected the best subjects, he wanted a more scientifically accurate method of making his choices.

Since, as already explained, I don't really believe in hypnotism anyway I prefer to concentrate on putting on a good show and I like to get good results from this preliminary test and the turning of the right hand seems to aid in this regard. However, I will let the reader decide which path he wishes to follow.

After you do this first test you follow up with this next one which seems to follow naturally on quite well. Again, you ask the volunteers to stretch out their hands in front of them but this time with the palms facing each other. They should hold the hands approximately 6 inches apart and you instruct them to do so. However, I often get a good laugh by approaching a very responsive subject who has reacted well in the previous test and physically move their hands apart even further saying, "In your case 12 inches apart."

The joke actually serves a deeper purpose since it kind of compliments the potential subject and will tend to encourage future compliance.

Again, you instruct them to close their eyes which have been open up to this point. Continue, "Imagine now that there are strong magnets between your palms. These magnets are so very strong that they are pulling your hands in closer and closer until they touch. Your hands are moving in, closing in, getting nearer and nearer until they touch. You cannot resist the influence. It is so very, very strong. Moving in, closing in. Getting nearer and nearer until they touch."

As you continue in this vein you will indeed see the hands moving in towards each other. As in the previous test some of the responses will be outstanding, some will be average and some will be sluggish. The people who respond well will tend to be your best subjects but as previously pointed out not always! It is, however, a fairly good guideline.

Continue, "Now as your hands are moving in you will see that the palms are beginning to touch together, they are beginning to stick together, they are sticking tight together, in fact they are sticking so tightly together that they are now stuck, stuck together. They are stuck so tightly together that you cannot separate them no matter how hard you try. They are stuck tight."

Some of the hands will indeed stick together with the palms touching. I often get a laugh when I approach a few subjects

Waking Suggestion On Stage

who are a bit slow in responding and I actually physically push the hands together! It does stop me having to wait all night!

Continue, "Your hands are stuck so tightly together that they are glued together, bonded together and you cannot pull your hands apart no matter how hard you try. Try hard, try very hard but the more you try the more they seem to stick. They stick tight, tight, tight together and you cannot separate them."

By this time a goodly portion of your subjects will seem to be struggling to get their hands apart. You can say "My, how they shake, how they tremble! It is due to the law of reversed effort. The more you try and separate them the more they stick tight, tight together." And so on and so forth. You will find the spectacle of the volunteers trying to open their hands is extremely amusing to the audience.

Continue by saying, "On the count of three your eyes will open (remember that up to this point they have been closed) and your hands will still be stuck. You will not be under hypnosis but your hands will be. One, two, three-open your eyes but your hands are still stuck, glued and bonded. You just cannot separate them!"

Eventually, when you have milked the situation dry you decide to end the test by saying, "All right, on the count of three the influence will all be gone. One, two, three-it's all gone, it's all gone and you are now able to take your hands apart" At this point they will release themselves although you may get the odd one or two that don't. They will be stuck together so tightly that they just cannot release themselves and this will add even further to the merriment of the audience. When this happens you simply handle the situation in exactly the same that I described earlier when the identical situation occurs with the magnetic fingers and the hand locking test. That is that you get them to gradually relax and take the hands apart on an individual basis.

By this time you will have had a chance to sum up your volunteers and it is time to decide who you will keep and who will have to leave the stage. Common sense will help you to figure this out. Generally, you will send back people who have not responded well to the tests. However, you will also eliminate people who have a bad attitude or people who show off. You will decide if people are liable to play along with things too much and exaggerate with such excess that they will spoil the show and you will likewise send back people whom you feel are not suitable subjects by reason of appearance, health or odd behavior. Actually, it is pretty easy to figure out who to keep and who to send back after a little experience of dealing with all the types that come up on stage.

An important point is that you can pick and choose with great abandon if hordes of people come up on stage to eagerly volunteer. However, in cases where a slow response occurs in volunteers marching up to the stage or they come up in dribs and drabs then it would behoove you to be very careful about whom you send back or even if you should send back anybody. Sometimes I will keep unsuitable subjects on stage because there has been such a poor response in volunteers coming forward that I cannot take the chance of sending anyone back in case I end up with nobody.

Occasionally the volunteers are such poor subjects that I just send them back but there are also other occasions when audience reaction might be a trifle sluggish and if I eliminate further people on stage there will be nobody left. My policy is that if people have to be eliminated because of poor response I will always keep at least 3 people on stage. That is the line where I draw the limit. I refuse to work with less that this number on stage and whether or not they are good subjects they will have to remain.

One little word of advice though. When people are dismissed get the audience to give them a round of applause as they go back to their seats. You want them to be on your side when they are part of the audience and no longer part of the show itself. You take the sting out of the rejection by saying early on in the show, "If I send any of you back into the audience please do not be offended. It does not mean that you cannot be hypnotized. It simply means that I cannot do it tonight since not everybody can concentrate with the same intensity as everyone else."

It is now time to commence the hypnotic induction with the remaining volunteers. This will be described in the next chapter.

CHAPTER SIX
The Hypnotic Induction

This is now the crux of the show. It is crunch time. The next few minutes can make or break you. It is time for the volunteers to enter what is known as the hypnotic state. This is what they came up for. It can also be the most fascinating phase of the show. At least for me anyway. The first time I saw a stage hypnosis demonstration this is the bit where my jaw dropped. It was quite something to see people who a moment ago were hale and hearty gradually drift into another world.

However, before you commence this make sure that nobody has any sharp objects on them that they could scratch or injure themselves on. It is also advisable for them to remove any spectacles. You take these and put them on a table to one side. After the show you return them. You also ask them to remove any chewing gum and you provide them a tissue for the use of such.

I have generally found it wise to make a few preparatory statements first that I address to the volunteers.

I say: "Let me explain what is about to happen to you during the next few moments. After all it is your minds that I am playing with.

When you are hypnotized you are not asleep. You are fully aware of what is going on. What I would describe as an altered state of consciousness rather than sleep. For example, if a dog was to bark or a phone were to ring you would hear it but you would detach yourself from it."

"People say to me what happens if I don't wake up? Well, it is impossible not to wake up. If I drop dead from heart failure while you are under hypnosis you won't be left sitting there for the rest of your life in a trance! The very worst than can happen is that you lapse into normal sleep and wake up in the ordinary way. If a fire breaks out in the building it doesn't mean that you will have to sit here waiting patiently to burn! Your subconscious mind will wake you up very quickly and you will run like heck just like everyone else!"

After making these remarks you tell your subjects that you are about to commence the hypnotic induction but you also warn the audience to be as quiet as possible while you are doing this. You accomplish this by saying the following, "We are about to commence the hypnotic induction and I would ask for complete silence over the next few minutes while we do this. By all means laugh, talk and enjoy yourselves once we have our volunteers under, in fact the stronger the audience response the stronger the hypnotic response, but for the next few moments please be as quiet as possible and give our volunteers the same courtesy you would expect if the positions were reversed."

Once you have the audience quiet you start the induction. I usually start by asking the volunteers to stare at some object such as a bright light on the ceiling. I call this an "object of fixation" which sounds vaguely scientific! Always remember that the more technical sounding terms you use the greater your credibility providing you don't overdo it!

I usually say something like the following:

"Make yourselves comfortable and keep your feet flat on the floor. Rest your hands on your knees so they do not touch."

"Stare at that light and as you do so you begin to find that your eye muscles are beginning to weaken and you want to close them. Your eyelids are becoming tired and heavy. Tired and heavy. In fact, they feel so tired and so heavy that you want to close them. Well, on the count of three you can close your tired eyes down tight, tight together. One. It's a strain looking at that light. Two. You really want to close your tired eyes down. Three. Close your eyelids down. That's it. Let them close down. If by chance they haven't closed down then close them anyway."

"And now you are finding that your eyelids are beginning to stick tight, tight together. They are sticking so tightly together that they are beginning to bond together and glue together and you cannot open them. Try, try hard. You cannot open them."

"All right now. Forget about your eyes and go to sleep. Take a deep breath. Hold the breath. Hold the breath. Now let it go. We'll do that again. Take a deep breath. Hold the breath, hold the breath. Now exhale letting all tension go. How good you feel, how fine you feel, how calm you feel. Nothing can bother you, nothing can disturb you. You feel so good.

Take a deep breath. Inhale slowly. Pause. Now exhale slowly. Once more, inhale slowly. Pause. Exhale slowly. Let all the stress go."

"Breathe deep. Breathe very deep. Breathe deep and go to sleep. Every breath sends you down deeper to sleep. Deeper to sleep. And your head is relaxing now. Let your head fall forward onto your chest. Drop it forward onto your chest and go to sleep. Go to sleep now."

"Now I'm placing your hand on the top of your head. Press your hand tightly to the top of your hand when I place it there. Press your hand in tightly to your head. Your hand is now pressing so tightly to your head that you cannot pull your hand away from your head no matter how hard you try. Try. Try hard. Try very hard. You cannot pull your hand away no matter how hard you try."

At this point you have made your way briskly along the group placing their right hand flat on the top of each head. Note the limpness of the arm as you do this. The limper the arm the more likely you are going to get good results from the owner of the arm. Conversely, the stiffer the arm the more effort that particular person will have to make to enter the state of hypnosis.

You should also find that a goodly percentage of your volunteers will indeed find it hard to remove the hand from the head. If, however, you find that the subjects free the hand it may be wise to consider them sending back into the audience.

You will have to use your own judgement here since difficult people sometimes comply once you get things going.

Continue: "Forget about your hands now. When I count to three your hand will drop like a dead weight limply into your lap and when it hits your lap you will go down twice as deep as you are now. One, two, three! Twice as deep as you are now!"

Study the reaction of the subjects here. If you see people whose hands drop with great abandon you will know that these will probably be your best subjects.

"I am going to count down from ten down to one and with each count you will drift down deeper and deeper to sleep."

"Ten. A wave of relaxation passes over you. You feel yourself falling, falling down asleep.

Nine. Your head feels like lead. So heavy as you sink further and further, deeper and deeper down.

Eight. Down, down to sleep. Hearing only my voice. Thinking of nothing but deep relaxing sleep.

Seven. Your arms are like lead. Heavy lead as you sink further and further down."

At this point I usually lift their arms and let them drop down to their sides. If they drop down like heavy lead I know I have got some live ones!

"Six. Your whole body feels like lead. So heavy as you sink deeper and deeper into profound sleep.

Five. You are halfway there. Halfway down. Down asleep.

Four. Blackness and darkness. Hearing only my voice. Thinking about nothing but deep relaxing sleep.

Three. Asleep. Deep, deep asleep. Thinking about nothing but deep deep sleep.

Two. You are falling through space and time. Feeling so relaxed and feeling so good.

One. You are almost there. Almost down. Down asleep.

Zero. Asleep. Deep asleep."

At this point you should have the subjects about to fall all over the place! You will be able to tell how far gone they are just by looking at them. Some of them will be slithering almost onto their neighbor or slumped right down in their chairs in obvious hypnosis. This is extremely fascinating to the audience and you can actually see people in the crowd with jaws dropping at the impossibility of the phenomena.

"When I clap my hands on the count of three you will go down twice as deep as you are now. One, two, three! Twice as deep as you are now!

When I clap my hands again on the count of three you will go down 4 times as deep as you are now. One, two, three! Four times as deep as you are now!

When I clap my hands on the count of three you will go down ten times as deep as you are now. One, two, three! Ten times as deep!"

Every time you clap you will see a deepening of the trance state and indeed it is quite uncanny. By this time they will be well under the influence and in fact may even be about to fall off their chairs! You can stop this happening by simply saying, "You will not fall off your chair" However, sometimes you actually DO want them to fall off their chairs because it looks so spectacular! You have to make sure that they do not hurt themselves when they do this and indeed many hypnotists will not let them fall because of safety concerns. However, there are times you can do this safely judging on the age and agility of the volunteers. However, you should temper things by saying "If you should happen to fall off your chair you will slither like a snake so that you do not hurt yourself." Then help them down. Or if you have an assistant helping you in the show, he or she can help to lower the person gently onto the ground.

Incidentally an assistant can be a decided asset to a show and I will devote some space to this later.

At this point I continue the induction by saying "When I shake you by the hand you will go down a hundred times as deep as you are now" Shake each person by their hand and give them a light shake and pull to one side. If you want them to fall to their left you shake their right hand and if you want them to fall to their right you shake their right hand. They will often fall onto the next person and land in their lap! Be very careful with safety when you do this. Make sure that nobody falls between the chairs. You can also shake the hand straight down and if you do this they will not tilt to one side but often bend forward with their heads between their legs.

At this point your volunteers are suitably in trance and you can continue with the show. You will find that some volunteers react very well with great abandon and some will be utterly useless. Then of course you will have the people who take a middle ground. Not overly animated but not too bad either. You dismiss the people that you deem unsuitable. These will be people who are not hypnotized and are refractory subjects. Whisper to them that they need to leave the stage and put your fingers to your lips to indicate that they should leave quietly so as not to disturb the "sleeping" subjects.

You now have a committee of hypnotized volunteers on stage and the fun is about to start in the next chapter!

CHAPTER SEVEN
On With The Show!

At this point you have a bunch of people who have dropped down like flies on the stage, perhaps one or two of them on the floor and the rest slumped down in their seats and maybe lying on top of each other.

I normally continue: "All hypnosis is self hypnosis. I don't hypnotize you. I just help you to hypnotize yourselves. And I am going to make you a promise. I promise that I won't get you to do anything that you don't want to do. I will ask your permission before every experiment"

This technique will remove any fear from the subjects that you will embarrass them and it makes you look good to the audience. In addition, it will help with the smooth running of the show.

At this point I like to introduce small effects of bodily sensation which don't require too much movement but enough that the subjects get used to following your suggestions. You start with the milder stuff then gradually graduate to the more outlandish feats of hypnosis.

Hot Cold And Itchy

I say, "In a few moments you are going to feel very hot, then very cold, then very itchy. Hot cold and itchy. If I have your agreement to this then please nod your head." This technique of asking permission from the volunteers is a very useful one for a stage hypnotist. It gives the subject warning of what you are about to do. Moreover, it extracts a commitment in advance from the volunteers to do as you require. Watch the reactions. Once you get the nods of the head then you proceed thus: "As you sleep warm, relaxed and comfortable you begin to feel an amazing sensation all over your body and you can actually control the temperature surrounding you. And as you sleep you begin to find this place to be very warm indeed. Phew! How warm it is! Very warm indeed. Fan yourself to get cool . You feel so hot! Hot! Hot! Loosen your tie, loosen your jacket -you feel so very warm. You can loosen your clothing but not too much –we want to keep this decent!"

You need to put that last line in otherwise you can get over-excited subjects actually doing a striptease! And of course, the line gives the less exuberant people an out so they don't have to undress. If you force people to do things they do not want to do they will wake up and refuse to cooperate further so you do have to be careful how you handle people and word things.

Continue in this vein and you will see the subjects fan themselves, loosen their clothing a little, possibly remove a jacket or even a shirt, squirm and generally try to make themselves more comfortable. Some of the subjects will of course react more strongly than the others and of course this will be evident in all the tests you do. You take note of these more enthusiastic subjects and make use of them in the more advanced tests which are to follow.

After you deem yourself to have had enough fun out of this you then alter your suggestions thus:

"OK. It's becoming much cooler. Much cooler. Cooler and cooler still. In fact it's becoming quite cold in here. Brrr! Quite cold indeed. In fact it's becoming quite chilly in here. Bundle up! Snuggle up! It's FREEZING in here!" Emphasize the word "freezing" and continue, "It is really cold in here. There is an icy cold wind outside and someone left the door open. It's FREEZING! What idiot left the door open and made this place so cold? And the person next to you is twice as warm as you are! It's not fair! They are twice as warm!" The last suggestion of them being "twice as warm" can often make the more animated subjects huddle together for warmth and this can get a great reaction from the audience.

The subjects at this point will act as if they are really cold. They will put back on any clothes they have taken off in the sequence when they felt hot and will do it very quickly if they are the more suggestible subjects. They will curl up with the cold and as already mentioned often snuggle up to the person next to them for warmth. The audience will howl at this.

After you have had your fun with this proceed thus, "All right, it's warming up now. It's not cold anymore. In fact, the room is the perfect temperature to relax and sleep in. Relax and sleep in. You feel so comfortable and relaxed. You feel great." The subjects will now act in a very relaxed manner.

You continue by saying, "And now we are going to try something that we have done before. The itching test. And not only will you feel it, members of the audience who are not even hypnotized will also feel it. But on stage the feeling will be intensified and you will want to scratch on the count of three. One! Two! Three! Scratch that itch away! You feel so very itchy, itchy, itchy! Scratch that itch." The subjects will scratch away in great abandon. When you want more action simply exclaim, "Bugs and fleas! Bugs and fleas!" or, "Ants in the pants! Ants in the pants!"

The audience will split their sides laughing but do not keep up this test for too long as it is not wise to make the volunteers uncomfortable for too long a time.

Now you say, "I have some ointment here that will make the itching go away. Put the ointment on! Put it on!" Run up and down the line or the people who may be on the floor and hand them some imaginary ointment. You will be amazed to see them take it and apply it vigorously to the itchy part of the body. Miraculously you will find that the itching will subside particularly if you say, "The itching has all gone now. All gone. Your skin feels smooth and pleasant, smooth and pleasant."

At this point I usually direct applause to the subjects by addressing the audience thus: "Our volunteers have done very well haven't they, ladies and gentlemen? Give them a big round of applause!"

The audience will applaud thus encouraging the volunteers to continue responding well as already explained in chapter four.

Hawaii Sequence

Continue, "In fact they have done so well that they deserve a reward. Do you think they deserve a reward?"

Usually the audience will yell out, "Yes!"

Continue, "What should I give them as a reward? Any ideas?" Then you act as if a thought had just struck you, "I know. A holiday! Perhaps they would like to go on holiday. Do you think they would like to go on holiday?"

The audience should yell out, "Yes!" You continue, "Let me find out if they really want to go on holiday." Turn around and address the volunteers. "Would you like to go on holiday? If you do, the way you signal it to me is to raise your leg in the air. And the higher you raise your leg the more I will know you want to go on holiday. Would you like to go on holiday?" The subjects will raise their legs in the air. Continue, "How much would you like to go on holiday?" They will raise the legs even higher and it will be quite a comic sight. Eventually you tell them to bring their legs back down to the floor.

Continue: "OK. We'll send you on a holiday." Address the audience now and ask them, "Where shall I send them? Any ideas?" The audience will call out various places and someone (if not the majority) will probably call out "Hawaii". Of course, if you are doing the show outside North America they may well say somewhere else. I usually use Hawaii. You address the volunteers and continue, "OK. We're going to send you all to Hawaii. If you would like to go to Hawaii then raise your leg in the air." They will then raise their legs in the air just like they did before and the repetition will make it even funnier. Tell them to replace their legs on the floor and continue in the following vein: "OK. We'll send you all to Hawaii. You're really going to like it. It will be beautiful weather and a very lovely place. We'll be there on the count of 5. Get ready for the trip. It will be very quick. There will be no jet lag. All your luggage will already be in the hotel when we get there. And all your friends back home will be freezing in the middle of winter while you are in beautiful Hawaii. They will be so-o-o jealous!"

Continue, "OK. We're going to Hawaii now. We'll be there on the count of five. Relax. One- we're on our way. Two-the trip is very fast and you are so excited. Three- it won't be long now. Four-you're nearly there. Five-we're in Hawaii! You are on the beach in Hawaii. It's so beautiful and the weather is great! Stretch out on the beach –you're having a great time!"

At this point the volunteers will either stretch out in their chairs in a very relaxed position or if they are on the floor, they will stretch right out as if they are actually on a beach. It is quite amazing to see. Some of them will actually slither from their chairs right down to the floor to take full advantage of the imaginary beach! Watch out for their safety, however, if they slither from their seats and be prepared to help them or let your assistant do it if you use one.

I should also mention here that on occasion you may be performing on a high stage which can affect the visibility of the audience not being able to see subjects who may be lying on the floor. It is good to be aware of this and use your discretion as to how long you wish them to lay there or even if you wish them to lay there at all. Of course, if you perform on floor level as you will often do then this situation will not arise and you don't have to worry about it.

Continue, "Beautiful weather. Beautiful sunshine. The waves of the ocean are in the distance and the seagulls are overhead. You can hear those seagulls. You feel so good and so relaxed and having a wonderful time"

"Wait a minute! Those seagulls are a bit mucky! They are dropping mess on you! Disgusting! Ugh! Wipe it off! Wipe it off! They should do something about those birds. They have diarrhea and are quite disgusting."

At this point the audience will be quite astounded to see the volunteers getting agitated at the supposed mess of the seagulls. Your subjects will be desperately wiping off the "mess" and acting quite upset about it. They can usually get quite animated in the process of doing this.

However, you do not keep up the discomfort too long and bring it to an end by saying, "Don't worry. I'll get rid of the birds. When I count to three and clap my hands the birds will all fly away. One! Two! Three! (clap your hands) Look! They're all flying away now. We've got rid of them!" However, the relief of the subjects is short lived when you continue, "Oh no, they're coming back! They are getting in your hair! Up your pants leg! Under your jacket! Shake them out! Shake them away!" You will get great animation from the subjects as they try and get rid of the non-existent birds. You help the illusion by ruffling the hair of the participants. This is particularly effective with the long haired subjects. I sometimes use a broom to reach the subject's hair and ruffle it. This broom is used in a subsequent experiment which I shall explain later.

After a while you end the commotion by saying "I'll get rid of them. On the count of three they will all fly away and not bother you any more. I will clap my hands on the count of three and they will all be gone! One! Two! Three! (clap your hands) They've all gone away now! They won't be back! You don't need to worry about them. I'll make you a promise. The birds won't bother you anymore. No need to worry about the birds. Just relax and enjoy the sunshine. That's it. Stretch out on the beach. Lovely weather. Lovely sunshine. You're having a great time in Hawaii again."

At this point the subjects will all be relaxed again and stretched out on the beach enjoying themselves. But you spoil their fun again by saying, "We're having good weather but someone said it was going to rain. I don't think it will rain. But wait! I did feel a raindrop. Oh no! I feel more! It's beginning to rain a little heavier. And now it's really pouring down! It's pouring with rain! Get some cover! We've got to get some cover! We're getting really drenched! Get some cover! Get some cover!"

The subjects will all now be desperate to find some cover. I assist them in this by throwing out various cloths I have stored on a table at the side of the performing area. They will cover themselves with these and the sight is very funny indeed. Sometimes if the subject is wearing a jacket they will remove it and place it over their heads to protect themselves from the rain. Often people will scurry under one of the chairs for cover and I will often encourage this by whispering to individual volunteers to do just that. I will whisper, "Get under the chair" and of course they comply and the audience will be in stitches.

As I suggested earlier the more the audience reacts the more the subjects will become animated. The stronger the audience response the stronger the hypnotic response. This is a useful thing to remember throughout your show.

I then continue the fun by exclaiming, "The storm is getting worse. Thunder and lightning. Thunder and lightning. It's the worst thunderstorm they have had in Hawaii for 30 years! You feel so wet!" This makes the volunteer react with even more vehemence and animation.

I now rescue everyone from their predicament by exclaiming, "It's stopped raining! It's all over! The sun is out! You don't need to worry about the rain any more! You can come out from under your cover now!" The "wet" subjects come out into the "dry" weather now. They crawl out from under the chairs or come out from their covers whether the cover be a cloth thrown earlier or perhaps a jacket or coat. You tell them to "Stretch out in the sun." and promise there will be no more rain to spoil the holiday.

You play this up for a while telling them that they can stretch out on the beach or laze around in their deck chairs in the warm pleasant sunshine. After all they deserve a reward for all the mayhem you have just been putting them through!

Eventually you inform them that it will soon be time for them to go home and that the aeroplane will be leaving soon.

Aeroplane Sequence

At this point you will probably have some subjects sitting in their seats and some lying on the floor. You have to somehow get those lying on the floor onto the seats. Since they think they are on the beach laying in the beautiful sunshine they might be a bit reluctant to move!

I usually handle it something like this. I say, "OK. I know you are all enjoying your wonderful holiday but it will soon be time to return home. We are going to take the aeroplane home. On the count of three you will be on the aeroplane waiting to return home. On the count of three those of you who are lying on the beach will get up and find your seat on the aeroplane. One, two, three! OK! Take your seats on the aeroplane! We are going home! Take your seats.!"

At this point some of those lying down will indeed get up off the floor and find a seat. However, it is quite possible that a few find it so comfortable that they won't make a move. Don't panic but just go up to them one at a time, touch the person on the shoulders and say, "You have to get on the plane now. It will be leaving soon. You don't want to miss the plane!". Sometimes I vary the procedure and say, "I am sorry sir, (or madam) you are not allowed to lie on the floor of the plane. Please take a seat." Of course, you conveniently omit to mention that a second ago they were on the beach rather than on the plane! Don't worry----it won't make the blindest bit of difference!

Anyway, once you get everyone on their seats you tell them that the plane is about to take off and that they should fasten their seatbelts and put their trays and chairs in the upright position. When they start to do this it will usually get a bit of a laugh from the audience.

You proceed now saying something like this, "OK. The plane is on the runway. It is starting to taxi on the runway. It will soon be about to take off. It will take off on the count of three. One, two, three! Zoom! A perfect take off!" You will find the subjects react to this by their facial expressions and moving back slightly as the imaginary plane takes off.

Incidentally, I am aware that some people are afraid of flying and I will often, before sending them off into the air, give suggestions and assurances that it will be a safe and pleasant flight. Of course, if you agree with my previously stated position that hypnosis doesn't exist, the subjects will know perfectly well that they are not on a plane anyway! Still, better safe than sorry and it doesn't take much time to assure everyone that the flight will be pleasant and safe so you might as well do it!

Sometimes when I have been in an overly cautious mood I have even, before starting the flight, asked if there are any volunteers who are afraid of flying and if so to indicate it by raising their hands. I then inform the scaredy cats that I will send them home by bus! I neglect to point out that Hawaii is an island and that buses can't fly over water but so far nobody has noticed this discrepancy!

Anyway, you continue in this vein, "Look out the window, beautiful sunshine, lovely scenery. We are flying low. You can see out of the window. In fact, you can see some friends that you met in Hawaii. Give them a wave. They can't see you but give them a wave anyway!" The subjects will wave to their imaginary friends which usually gets a laugh from the audience. However, you get an even bigger laugh when you follow up with, "Oh, you can also see some people down there that you met in Hawaii and you couldn't stand the sight of them. Really obnoxious. They can't see you but you can see them. So give them any kind of sign you wish. Go on! They can't see you anyway!"

Your volunteers will now give really borderline (and sometimes not so borderline) obscene gestures through the "window" at the imaginary people they see on the ground. This usually gets a very strong reaction of hilarity from the audience.

You continue the flight thus, "Oh, it is a very pleasant smooth flight. You feel so very comfortable. Oh wait a minute, there is a bit of turbulence! Up and down! Up and down! Very shaky! OK. OK. It is calming down now, calming down. No more turbulence—that's much better" The subjects will react accordingly. This is an effective sequence but I try not to draw out the turbulence aspect too long. The whole thing lasts only a few seconds in fact as I don't want to make my volunteers too uncomfortable.

Continue: "Oh, the flight is very smooth and pleasant now. Smooth and ever so pleasant. OK. It's time to have a drink now! We are serving the drinks on the plane. What drink would you like? It is your holiday----you can have any drink you like. I'll tell you what---we have a new special drink here. It is called giggle water. Once you take a sip of this you won't be able to stop giggling. Here you are. Have a good laugh—have a good giggle! You can't stop giggling. The more you drink the more you giggle! Go on—have a good laugh---you are really having a great time!"

Saying the above you go to the various subjects and offer them an invisible "drink". Laugh and giggle yourself to some degree to set an example and aid the suggestion. Once you have milked the situation to your satisfaction you proceed as follows:

"OK, you've finished your drink and you feel very content. You are really enjoying yourself. There is only one problem. There is an awful body odour coming from the person next to you. What a stink! You don't want to say anything to that person. You want to be polite. But what a stink!"

At this point the volunteers (or at least some of them!) will start to grimace and put their hands to their nose, often looking disdainfully at the person next to them. This will result in audience laughter which will encourage the reactions even more. You then go up to one of the stink affected subjects and ask what is the matter. The response tends to vary here; some volunteers will merely point to the person next to them and some will not just point but say out loud, "he stinks" which will produce quite a bit of laughter from the audience!

You then rectify the situation by announcing, "OK. We'll sort that out. I have some very strong air freshener here. Let me spray it round the cabin! There we are! The air is fresh again. There is no stink any more. You can completely relax and enjoy the flight again. Oh, it is a very pleasant flight and you are having a really good time!" You will find that the subjects will relax accordingly and appear in a more pleasant mood.

You now continue on to the movie scene. This is quite an amusing part of the show which produces both laughter and sadness from the assembled subjects.

"OK everybody. It will soon be time for the movie. We are going to show a movie on the aeroplane. Sometimes the movie will be very funny and sometimes it will be very sad. But you are really going to enjoy the movie. Get ready for the movie now. On the count of three you will open your eyes remaining firmly in trance and you will see in front of view a giant movie screen. You are really excited about the movie. You really want to see it. You've heard all about it. OK. On the count of three you will see it. Get ready! One! Two! Three! Eyes open and there's the movie!" The subjects will now open their eyes and look at the imaginary screen. The reason you have delayed things by telling them to get ready and that they will be excited to see the movie, plus counting up to three, is because you need to give them time to adjust for what is about to happen. They will react better if you do this.

Continue, "Oh look! There is a clown slipping on a banana skin! It is so funny! Everyone is laughing at him! So, so funny! Oh, now look at this! I don't believe it. There is an old lady jumping up and down on a trampoline. She is 99 years old and jumping up and down. The funniest thing you have ever seen! Up and down, up and down. Oh no! I don't believe what she is doing now! She used to be a striptease dancer! She is taking off all her clothes and jumping up and down, up and down! You don't have to look if you don't want to but if you do look it will be quite a sight! The funniest thing you have ever seen!"

Your subjects will react accordingly and start laughing. The audience will add to the laughter which in turn will increase the merriment of the volunteers. In other words, the audience will be laughing at the laughter thus creating more laughter! As I have mentioned in a previous chapter the more the audience responds the more the subjects will respond. This is because the power of suggestion is at work. Conversely if there is a lack of response from the audience there may well be a lack of response from the subjects. Thus, the power of suggestion can be a double-edged sword. It can work for you but if you are not careful it can also work against you. Thus, it is important to encourage the audience to respond as much as you can.

Anyway, you now change the mood from laughter to sadness by continuing thus, "Oh wait a minute! The movie is not funny anymore. It is becoming quite sad. The mother has lost her baby. She can't find her baby. It is very, very sad. I hope she finds her baby!" Your volunteers will now react with sadness and may even appear to cry. (or at least pretend to!). At this point I normally hand out tissues to the subjects to help them with their crying and sadness!

Anyway, you add to the misery by saying, "Oh dear, the wicked landlord has thrown her out of the apartment and she is walking through the snow with her two starving children. It is very, very cold and she has lost her baby! It is so, so very sad." At this point your volunteers will be crying and your audience will be laughing!

Suddenly, you bring the story to a happy ending by continuing, "Oh wait a minute! She's found her baby!" You will actually see expressions of relief from your subjects at hearing this welcome news especially when you continue by saying, "Oh, she's got a new landlord! She is living in a luxury apartment! All the children are happy! Oh look! There's that funny old lady again! Jumping up and down on the trampoline! Up and down! Up and down! The funniest thing you have ever seen!" This transformation from sadness to happiness is quite a contrast and very effective to the audience.

You now finish off the scenario by declaring, "Oh—the movie is over now. All over! It was a wonderful movie. Just sit back and enjoy the flight. We will be coming in to land soon. Lovely sunshine outside. You feel so relaxed and so good"

After a short pause you now prepare them for the landing thus: "OK. We are coming in to land now. You have had a great time but the journey is nearly over. Fasten your seatbelts and put your chairs and trays in the upright position. We are getting lower now. Look out the window and you will see the green fields underneath. Oh, there is the airport. We are coming in to land. Woosh! A perfect landing! Give the pilot a bit round of applause!" At this point give the audience a signal to applaud thus encouraging the volunteers to do likewise.

Revolving Arms Sequence

Continue, "OK. You have had a wonderful holiday. On the count of three you will open your eyes remaining firmly in trance" I usually repeat the phrase thus, "On the count of three you will open your eyes remaining firmly in trance and we will proceed to more advanced experiments. One---getting ready to do it. Looking forward to it. Two---eyes beginning to open. Three----eyes open remaining firmly in trance and look at me and only me."

You now stand facing the subjects with your arms parallel to each other as in the photograph.

Instruct the subjects, "Put your arms parallel to each other like this. Put them parallel to each other like this" Incidentally, I often repeat certain phrases to make sure the suggestion sinks in.

Once the subjects follow the above suggestion continue thus, "Now let your arms revolve around each other just like this."

You demonstrate what you mean by revolving your own arms around each other and continue, "Now close your eyes. Now as you revolve your arms around each other you find they are beginning to pick up speed. This is known as automatic movement in the hypnotic state. They are going faster and faster. Faster and faster! And you won't be able to stop them! They are going on their own accord now! Faster and faster! Faster and faster! When I clap my hands, your arms will go twice as fast! Twice as fast!" Clap your hands and this will indeed speed up the action even more!

The more excitement you can generate in your voice the better. This very excitement will also encourage the action from your subjects. Once you get all the arms going round and round each other you up the action by saying, "The faster they go the more the audience will applaud! The faster they go the more the audience will applaud!" Again, note the repetition in the phrasing. You will now find that the audience will applaud and this will increase the reactions of the volunteers.

Incidentally, I have once seen it advised that you should warn the volunteers not to hit themselves on the nose while conducting this experiment! I have never followed this admonition and fortunately it has never happened yet after hundreds of shows. I don't think it every will either but there it is for what it is worth!

Sometimes I will protract the scenario of the applauding audience by promoting a competition among the subjects thus, "Ladies and gentlemen. Let us see who moves their arms the fastest. I will go to each person in turn and I would like you to give the strongest applause to the person you think is going the fastest"

You now go behind each volunteer and put your hand above each person's head and ask, "How much applause does this man get?" going down the line saying, "What about this lady?" and so on. The audience will clap weakly over the less active subjects and enthusiastically over the most animated ones. Take good notice of the volunteers who get the most applause since they will be the ones you can use later in the show for individual and more dramatic suggestions.

Once you ascertain the winner of this little contest announce, "This fellow is the winner. Give him a great big round of applause!"

You now continue, "When I clap my hands your arms will freeze dead in the air. When I clap my hands, your arms will freeze dead in the air. One! Two! Three! (Clap your hands). Look! Your arms are frozen dead in the air! You cannot move your arms no matter how hard you try! Try! Try hard! You cannot move your arms!"

This is a very dramatic demonstration which looks a lot better live than described in cold print! I have always felt a strange glow of satisfaction when the whirling hands dramatically come to a stop and are stuck parallel to each other in mid air!

Continue, "You cannot move your arms until I clap my hands and off they will go again. One, two three (clap) and off they go again! Faster and faster! When I clap my hands again, they will go in the reverse direction! Reverse direction!" Suddenly the subjects will stop in mid stream and rotate their arms in the reverse direction which is quite a sight to see! Once you have milked this to a satisfactory extent you now continue the action by exclaiming, "On the count of three your arms will go any way they want to go! Backwards, forwards, zig zag, inside out---any way they want to go! One! Two! Three! Any way they want to go!"

At this point the volunteers will flail wildly with their hands in all sorts of directions which will create great hilarity among the audience. Once you feel this has gone on long enough you calm things down by saying, "OK, go back down to sleep now, back down to sleep. Relaxed and comfortable" Your subjects will follow this suggestion accordingly.

Canary Test

You now continue, "OK. I am going to count up to five and when I do so you will open your eyes remaining firmly in trance. In a moment we are going to proceed to a more advanced experiment. It is called hallucination in the hypnotic state. It will be very interesting even from a scientific point of view.

On the count of five you will open your eyes remaining firmly in trance and you will see in front of you the most beautiful canary bird you have ever seen. You will love it very much. It will mean everything to you. You won't let anyone touch it or harm it in any way. You love it so much. Such a beautiful canary. So special. OK. One. You are looking forward to seeing the canary. Two. Put your left hand out now to receive the bird. Three. You can feel it landing on your hand. So lovely. It will hop from hand to hand. It will fly on your shoulder. It will move around quite a bit. You love it very much. Four. Eyes beginning to open. Five. And there's the bird! Play with it!"

At this point there will be quite a bit of laughter from the audience which will encourage the subjects to play things up to their full extent. They will pet the invisible canary and "see" it hopping around on their hands and shoulders. You can even give a suggestion that one or two of the birds are flying under the chair but eventually returns to the hands of the subjects. Of course, the subjects will look under the chairs while all this is going on and the audience will love it!

This is the point where things get really dramatic! You continue, "On the count of three the birds will fly away and you will try to catch them! And I will help you catch them! One, two three! The birds are flying away!"

At this point the "birds" will fly away and the subjects will start running after them. They will run around the stage searching for their imaginary birds and often run into the audience to find them. Now a lot depends on where you are performing as to how you handle this. If you are performing on a stage you don't want your volunteers falling off the stage or in the case of overly exuberant young people even jumping off the stage! You also don't want people bumping in to each other while running around. There are times when you may deem it wise to control things by issuing a suggestion such as, "When you chase after your canary you will make sure you do not hurt yourself. You will not fall off the stage or bump into anyone".

You also have to make sure that everyone returns to the stage. It is possible that someone might take a trip into the audience to find their canary but not come back! I still remember doing a show once at an outdoor event and after the canary chasing had subsided, I noticed one volunteer was missing and had not returned to the stage. I scanned the audience but couldn't see her anywhere. I belatedly announced to the crowd that subjects should return on stage as they were still in a hypnotic state. Mind you, I strongly suspect the real reason they don't return is that they know full well they aren't "hypnotized" and don't feel like acting daft on stage anymore! Not that I am of a cynical frame of mind of course!

Anyway, with regard to the above incident I was about to give up trying to find the missing subject when members of the audience pointed to a cramped space underneath the stage area. I went down to have a look and was astonished to see a woman crawling underneath the stage in the dirt trying to find the missing canary! I realized this was a situation fraught with peril and somehow I had to get her out from beneath the stage before I got sued for something or other!

I yelled to her through the microphone, "Oh, I have a message for the lady who is underneath the stage. I have found your canary. It is here in my hands safe and sound. You can come out now! I have your canary! But you must come out slowly and carefully so you do not hurt yourself, slowly and carefully, slowly and carefully! Accordingly, she did crawl out of her restricted space and I heaved a big sigh of relief. The audience laughed and applauded the entire time while all this was going on but I was sweating bullets!

Anyway, once you have extracted all the fun out of the canary chasing, you bring the excitement to an end by suggesting something along these lines, "OK. You all have your canaries now. They are no longer flying away. Do you have yours? OK. What about you? OK. Everybody has their canaries. Relax and sit down. Relax and sit down"

The volunteers are now seated playing with their "canaries" once again. At this point I generally tell them to close their eyes and go back down to sleep again. You now approach your most responsive subject saying, "You have a lovely canary, don't you? You love it very much" You will get a positive response. You continue, "Did you know I am a magician? I have just learned a new magic trick. It is called the disappearing canary trick!" At this point the subject will look quite alarmed and try to protect the bird and show it in his body language. Nevertheless, you continue by saying in a menacing tone, "On the count of three I will clap my hands and your canary will disappear. One! Two! Three!" You now clap your hands and sneer, "Your canary has now disappeared!" Your subject will look quite distressed and bewildered. However, you do not prolong the agony and quickly go on to say, "Don't worry, I will make it come back again. I know where it is" You continue, "I

On With The Show!

have heard that there is someone in here who has been stealing canaries. I have been trying to find out for days who it is. Now I know. And you will get the canary back"

At this juncture you now point to some hapless member of the audience and spout, "See that man there? He stole your canary! Go and demand your canary back!" Your subject will approach the accused canary thief, sometimes in quite a menacing manner so it would also be advisable to issue this suggestion, "You will not physically attack him!" This remark with result in laughter from the audience as well as stopping the action from getting out of hand!

Things will get quite hilarious at this point and you will have to play it by ear according to what happens. Generally, your subject will approach the poor innocent audience member and either ask politely or more likely aggressively demand to have the canary returned. I accompany him to make sure things don't get out of hand and my presence by his side encourages his responses.

The audience member may well react in different ways according to the circumstances. He or she might deny the possession of the bird or they might perhaps return the imaginary bird. If the latter happens, I usually step in and say, "That's the wrong one!" and keep the conflict going! I then advise, "Tell him that if he doesn't return the canary, you will call the police!" After playing this situation up for a while instruct the canary theft victim not to worry and we will find a policeman.

At this point you bring the subject back to the performing area where the rest of the hypnotized volunteers are. You select the most likely person of the group to be the policeman and say to the theft victim, "Look, that man there is a policeman. Oh dear, he is asleep on duty! What are we paying our taxes for?"

The above remark will get quite a laugh from the audience. However, by far the biggest laugh I ever got for saying "he is asleep on duty" was when I performed a show for a police association in front of an audience of real police officers!

Anyway, at this point you have to waken our police officer and put him to work. This is how you do it. You tap the sleeping "policeman" on the shoulder and suggest, "On the count of three you will awaken and become a policeman. You will be full of authority and very strict indeed. You will help this member of the public who has had a canary stolen. If you agree to this nod your head"

This head nodding technique has already been described in the "Hot, Cold and Itchy" sequence explained earlier in this section. It is a very useful technique since it gives the subject time to process the suggestion and once they do nod their head you know you are going to get cooperation.

Continue, "One, you are beginning to awaken. Two your eyes are starting to open. Three, eyes open remaining remaining in trance. You are now a policeman!"

At this point you turn to the "victim" and instruct him or her to tell the "policeman" the canary problem. You will probably get a response along the lines of the "victim" pointing to the audience member yelling, "he's got my canary and I want it back!"

Again this is a play by ear scenario. Probably what will happen at this point is that the "policeman" will approach the accused audience member accompanied by the "victim". I accompany both parties to the scene of the "crime" and location of the "suspect". One advantage of this is that my proximity to the three parties allows me to secretly communicate various suggestions to the subjects to enhance the entertainment depending on how circumstances evolve. This is done in a play by ear manner and is dependent on how the situation develops. It is done by speaking in a low voice so the subjects can hear you but out of the earshot of the audience.

The situation can develop in all sorts of ways depending on the personalities of the characters involved. It is a little difficult to give a precise description of what scenarios will develop. However, a typical situation might be that the "suspect" might deny he has the canary and an argument could develop. The "policeman" might be tactful or aggressive. Quite often the "thief" will return the canary. When that happens, I usually suggest quietly to the "policeman" that he tells the "thief" not to do it again. Sometimes when the canary is returned, I will butt in and say, "that's the wrong one—he gave you the wrong one!" and prolong the situation!

One thing I often do is say, "It's under his jacket" or if the subject is wearing a hat, say, "The canary is under his hat". This can often provoke the "victim" to grab the hat or open the offender's jacket. The whole scenario can become quite hilarious and of course a lot depends on how the scene will develop. You will have to use your imagination and off the cuff creativity when performing this skit since anything can happen!

However, in the end you make sure the canary has been recovered, the thief has been admonished and the officer of the law is given a big round of applause by the audience and returns to his seat along with the proud owner of the returned canary.

I should mention that this stolen canary sequence can present some difficulties if you are performing on a high stage to a large audience. That is because it is impractical for your subjects to go down into the audience to accost a victim who allegedly stole the canary. They have to go down some steps and the audience is too far away from the stage, thus making the trip a little too long. Another more major problem is that if you are performing before a large audience once you go offstage people can't really see properly what is going on and you are in great danger of losing the attention of the audience. The way you get around this is, rather than the subject going in to the audience, you simply use one of the other hypnotized participants on stage as the "canary thief". You will find this alternative a practical solution.

At this point you put everyone down to sleep again. Just tell them to close their eyes down and go back into sleep. You go down the row and say to each volunteer in turn, "Go back down to sleep". However, you also whisper to your three most responsive subjects, "When I touch you on the forehead you will go instantly asleep" You do this to set up for the "Instant Induction" stunt which I will describe later.

Once you get your subjects into a reasonable appearance of tranquility inform them that you are about to waken them all up again. You say something along these lines. "OK. I am going to wake you all up now on the count of five. You will feel full of vim, vitality and pep. You will feel fresh and relaxed. You will feel absolutely fine.

One-getting ready to awaken. Two-knowing you have done very well. Three-eyes beginning to open. Four-beginning to awaken. Five-wide, wide awake! Feeling great! Feeling fine!"

Your subjects are now awake. It is actually a good idea at this point of the show to give the volunteers a rest from the hypnotic trance.

At this point tell the audience to give your volunteers a big round of applause. As previously explained the more reaction and applause the subjects receive the more inclined they are to react well to your suggestions.

Continue, "Ladies and gentlemen. At this point I would like to demonstrate something known as instantaneous hypnosis. This is the fastest demonstration of hypnosis known today". You now approach one of the subjects you secretly primed to sleep when you touch their forehead. Ask, "How are you feeling?" When the subject responds suddenly touch the person's forehead and command, "Sleep!". Your volunteer will suddenly fall instantly into trance again! This will have an astonishing effect on the audience and is a very dramatic part of the show.

You now approach a second subject that you previously primed and direct their attention to the person you just instantaneously hypnotized and say, "Look at that! Have you ever seen anything like that in your life?" Your participant will probably laugh and say "no" whereupon you touch him or her on the forehead and exclaim "Sleep!" and he or she will go instantly down into a sudden trance in the same way the other person did. This will usually garner a lot of gasps and laughter from the audience. You now repeat this procedure with the third person you previously primed and that subject will also go into a sudden trance state! Audiences are usually quite startled by this very dramatic sequence.

You now address the audience thus, "Ladies and gentlemen. You have just witnessed spontaneous somnambulism. It does not happen very often but there are some individuals so suggestible that instant hypnosis can be induced"

This statement of course is a lot of tosh but it sounds very scientific and makes you look like an expert. Of course, the more you come across as an expert the more this assures the success of the show.

At this point you put the remaining subjects back down into hypnosis. You don't have to do the full induction here since the volunteers have already experienced the trance state (if there is such a thing) and will go "under" far more easily the second time around. All you have to do is shorten the induction drastically in the following manner. First you get the subjects to look at a prominent point in front of them or perhaps above them. I find a light of some sort to be quite useful in this regard. You then tell them that their eyes are becoming tired and heavy and they will want to close them. You do this in a similar manner to that described in the induction chapter of this book. Furthermore, you suggest to the three people you have already hypnotized by the instantaneous method already described that as they listen to your voice they will go even deeper.

Once the volunteers have their eyes closed you cut out most of the induction described in Chapter Six and start from the point when you count backwards from the number four thus:
"Four. Blackness and darkness. Hearing only my voice. Thinking about nothing but deep relaxing sleep.
Three. Asleep. Deep, deep asleep. Thinking about nothing but deep, deep sleep.

Two. You are falling through space and time. Feeling so relaxed and feeling so good.
One. You are almost there. Almost down. Down asleep.
Zero. Asleep. Deep asleep."

Once everyone is down to sleep you proceed as follows:

"You are now deep asleep. In a few moments you will open your eyes and look at the audience. You will be quite shocked to see that the entire audience will be buck naked. Now you don't have to look if you don't want to but if you do look it will be quite a sight. You will never have seen anything like it! However, whenever you hear me say the word 'reverse' the positions will be reversed and audience will have their clothes back on but you yourselves won't be wearing a stitch of clothing and you will try to get some cover so they can't see you not wearing anything. Then when I say 'back to normal' everything will be back to normal and everyone will have their clothes back on again. . If you agree to this nod your head"

As previously explained this head nodding is a very useful technique as it prepares the subjects for what is to come. It also gives you some assurance that your suggestions are going to be followed as well as gives you a warning as to any reluctance shown by individual volunteers.

You now continue, "OK. I am going to count up to three. One—there's something interesting happening in the audience. Two—you really want to have a look at it. Three—eyes opening remaining in trance. Look at the audience. What do you think of that?"

The subjects will now look at the "naked" audience and act accordingly. They might point at the audience derisively or look embarrassed. Perhaps someone will shield their eyes. There will usually be a variety of reactions according to the personalities of your volunteers. You can even play the situation up by approaching one or two of your subjects asking them what is wrong and you will often get hilarious responses.

Suddenly you call out "reverse" and then things will get quite chaotic! The subjects will start to look very alarmed, hide their private parts and try to get some cover. They will often duck under their chairs or hide behind stage curtains or furniture. On occasion you will sometimes get exhibitionist personalities parade their "nakedness" around to everyone which of course garners even bigger laughs from the audience. I usually have some large cloth materials handy that I throw out to selected subjects with which they cover themselves with very quickly.

Anyway, you bring all the hilarity to an end by suddenly exclaiming, "Back to normal! Back to normal!" whereupon your volunteers will look slightly startled especially when you follow up with, "Everything is OK. Everybody has their clothes back on!"

At this point I normally get the audience to applaud the volunteers. I have already explained why you do this with a certain amount of frequency during your performance. I now direct the participants to go deep down to sleep again after which I announce to the audience. "I am now going to conduct an experiment with this lady here". So saying, you approach a suitable female subject. You continue, "In a moment on the count of three, you will have in your arms the man of your dreams. You love him very much. You haven't seen him for such a long while. You will treat him with much affection. Not too much affection though since we want to keep this decent. OK. One----two----three---here you are! The man of your dreams!"

So saying you put a broomstick into her hands and this will provoke great hilarity from the audience as she hugs and kisses the broomstick in her arms!

Suddenly you announce, "Wait! I've found your canary! Here you are!". You hand over the invisible bird to your volunteer who will appear quite delighted over the matter.

Continue, "You've got the man of your dreams and your canary! Isn't that wonderful?" You will of course receive a positive response to this question. However, you spoil everything by announcing, "There is only one problem. The man of your dreams hates the canary! He says either the canary goes or he goes!"

The reaction varies here. Very often the woman will throw away the canary which of course gets a laugh. However, a much bigger laugh will occur if she does the reverse and throws the broomstick away and keeps the canary! In fact, I will often cue the subject under my breath so the audience can't hear to throw away the man of her dreams and to keep the canary instead! I just whisper, "Throw the broomstick away" and invariably this is what she will do and it will garner a huge laugh from the audience.

You now continue to a most effective post hypnotic suggestion test. You approach a lady who has proved to be a responsive subject, tap her on the shoulder and say, "We are going to try a most interesting post hypnotic experiment. Whenever this lady hears me say the word "hypnotism" and snap my fingers she will leap out her chair with a yell and shout, 'I'm the last of the Red Hot Mamas!"

Give her a chance to absorb this then continue with the head nodding technique thus, "If you agree to this then nod your head" On the rare occurrence that she doesn't nod her head you can simply go to another subject and repeat the same procedure.

Continue by selecting another responsive subject and tap him or her on the shoulder saying, "Whenever you hear me say the word 'hypnotism' and snap my fingers you will leap out of your chair and yell, 'the British are coming, the British are coming'. If you agree to this nod your head."

You now approach a third volunteer and you really have to make sure here that this person is a very responsive subject. You ask, "Do you know the words of the national anthem? Or part of it anyway? At least the first few lines?" If you get a negative response you can always abandon the attempt and try again with a different participant. However, you will usually find someone who will go along with things. You say, "Whenever I say the word "hypnotism" and snap my fingers you will stand up and sing the national anthem. Don't worry if you don't know the words. Just do the best you can and the audience will help you" Turn to the audience and say, "You will help her (or him) won't you ladies and gentlemen?" You will usually provoke a loud cheer from the crowd! This audience participation, as already explained previously, helps to increase the responses of the subject. Again you ask the volunteer to give a nod of the head to indicate acceptance of the suggestions.

You now approach a final likely subject and address that person thus, "You are now in charge of this event and in fact in charge of this very stage. You are full of authority and will not put up with any silliness. Whenever I snap my fingers and say the word "hypnotism" you will open your eyes remaining firmly in trance. If you see anyone acting like idiots you will immediately stand up and say in a loud voice, 'SHUT UP AND SIT DOWN YOU FOOLS!' Now if the audience laugh or make a noise you will tell the audience to be quiet otherwise you will call security. You will be in charge. If you agree to this nod your head"

Once you secure this agreement you now face the audience and address them directly, "Ladies and gentlemen. You have just witnessed an interesting phenomenon. In fact, I was in Montreal (name any city you like) recently and was on a radio show to discuss HYPNOTISM!" You raise your voice when you say "HYPNOTISM" and also snap your fingers to indicate the signal. On occasion it doesn't register and nothing happens. Don't panic and simply say the one word "HYPNOTISM" loudly again until your volunteers get the message. Oh, and don't forget to snap your fingers as an extra cue to set things off!

If you have done this correctly all hell will now break loose! One person will stand and shout "I am the best of the Red Hot Mamas!" Another will start screaming, "The British are coming!" Still another will stand up and start to sing the national anthem. In fact, the first two are both quite likely to do this several times and the third one will keep on singing. The person you put in charge of the stage will seem to become upset and tell the three disrupters to "Shut up and sit down you fools!"

At this point I get behind the appointed orderly and cue him quietly to tell the audience to stop making a noise. However, behind his back I signal to the audience by silently clapping my hands together to make even more noise! He will then get more annoyed by the audience noise and I will continue to secretly cue him with suggestions as to what to say. Such things as, "Settle down now" or "You should all know better" and "If you don't be quiet I will call security". This of course will make the noise even worse. While all this is going on your three other subjects will be yelling and singing so there will be quite a bit of mayhem going on.

Eventually you secure order by telling everyone to go back down to sleep again. You resume your interrupted speech and continue, "Sorry about that, ladies and gentlemen. As I was saying I was listening to the radio the other day and they were talking about HYPNOTISM"! Now snap your fingers at the same time you say "hypnotism" and all hell will break loose again!

This repeat of the actions will usually produce even more merriment than the first time! Sometimes I vary the procedure by using the national anthem sequence in a different part of the show. I do not use the other three volunteers this time and instead use it as an individual test. I approach the volunteer and suggest to him or her in the way already described to sing the national anthem. The subject will do so but this time you encourage the audience to join in. This will especially assist the volunteer if he or she forgets some of the words. It can be a very stirring part of your show to see the entire audience singing the national anthem led by your hypnotised subject!

OK. Now back to business. You restore order to the mayhem just described and all your hypnotized subjects go right back to sleep. Deepen the trance by the method already explained.

At this point you continue, "I am now going to show you how the hypnotic state can stimulate the imagination. In a moment when I count to three you will all stand up and become coffee percolators even to the extent of boiling over. Boiling and bubbling. One, you are beginning to boil and bubble, two you are taking on more heat. Heat! Three, standing up as a coffee percolator! Percolating! Percolating!"

The subjects will now all stand and become coffee percolators! It is quite a sight to behold and the audience will find it hilarious! After you have milked this to its full extent you continue, "OK relax! You are no longer a coffee percolator. On the count of three you will be a typewriter. One, two three! You are now a typewriter. Clickety click, clickety click. Typing away, typing away. You must get that letter done!"

The subjects react according to their own imaginations and the effect can be quite striking. You now continue, "OK. You are no longer a typewriter. On the count of three you will become a washing machine! One, two, three! You are now a washing machine! Spinning and turning, spinning and turning" The subjects will all start to spin and turn and this provokes an incredible amount of laughter from the audience. There is plenty of action and thrashing about which is quite astonishing to watch!

Continue, "On the count of three you will no longer be a washing machine. You will be a vacuum cleaner! One, two, three! You are now a vacuum cleaner! Zoom! Zoom! You have to get things clean!"

At this point your volunteers start to become vacuum cleaners according to their own imaginations. Some of them will even start to get down on the ground crawling on the floor to sweep up the dirt! If this happens don't worry since the next and final impersonation will make them stand up again!

Continue, "OK. I am now turning off the vacuum cleaner. I am switching it off. You are no longer a vacuum cleaner. On the count of three you will stand up (you say this especially to those on the floor) and become a tree. A mighty oak tree. One, two three! Your roots are sinking deep into mother earth. You are growing higher and higher as a tree. Your branches are reaching out towards the sky. You are a mighty, mighty oak tree!"

The preceding tree scenario may not sound like much in print but I can assure you that on stage in a live performance it is quite an impressive demonstration. Almost beautiful and inspiring in a weird sort of way! I recommend at this point that you encourage the audience to give a big round of applause to the "trees". I find that for some odd reason the audience will applaud this tree sequence quite forcefully.

And so ends the impersonation routine. A lot of stage hypnotists perform skits where the participants impersonate various celebrities and of course this can be very effective. I find the above sequence of impersonating imaginary objects to be just as good!

You now suggest to your subjects that they are no longer trees and that they return to their chairs on stage.

At this point you are nearing the end of your show. You have a stage full of hypnotized subjects and you have to unhypnotize them and get them back to their seats in the audience. This is how I personally do it.

I say, "Now, I'm going to wake you all up on the count of five. You will feel alert and refreshed. You will feel great. You will have something to tell your friends. And your friends will have something to tell you. (This last sentence gets a laugh from the audience). But you will have one tiny problem when you wake up. You will be stuck to your chair. You will pull and you will tug but you will not be able to get out of your chair no matter how you try. Until you hear me say the word 'hot'. When you hear me say the word 'hot' your chair will become so hot that you will leap out of your chair with a yell. Because your chair will be so hot."

"I will repeat the suggestion. When I count to five you will be wide awake but you will be stuck to your chair. Until I say, 'hot' and when I say, 'hot' your chair will become so hot that you will jump up with a yell. Then after that all suggestions

On With The Show!

from tonight will be removed. All suggestions will be removed. If you understand me nod your head." (Wait until they do).

You now continue with this very effective post hypnotic suggestion which will be an excellent climax to the show. You continue, "When you return to the audience there will be one tiny problem. I will ask if anyone has left anything on stage and when you hear me ask that you will find that your belly buttons are missing! You cannot find your belly buttons! You will be quite upset that you cannot find it! You will ask people in the crowd, 'has anyone seen my belly button'. You will get very agitated and angry that you cannot find your belly button! Until I say 'Back to normal! Your belly button is back' and then your belly button will be back and all suggestions will be removed. After all we don't want you all going to work tomorrow without your belly buttons!"

You repeat the above post hypnotic suggestions to make sure everyone understands what they have to do. You tell them that when they wake up they will be stuck to their chairs. When you say "hot" their chairs will become hot and they will leap up with a yell. When they return to the audience you will ask if anyone has left anything behind on stage. When they hear that they will find their belly buttons are missing. When you say that their belly buttons are back they will find that their belly buttons have indeed returned and all suggestions are removed.

You now continue "OK. It's time to get up now. You have had a wonderful time under hypnosis but it's time to get up. One, you are beginning to awaken. Two, I am going to give you a few moments to adjust. Three, coming back to the here and now. Four, beginning to open your eyes. Five. Wide awake! Wide awake!"

You have now woken everyone up but you have planted what is known as a post hypnotic suggestion which they will feel impelled to follow. The suggestion of being stuck to their chairs and then the chairs becoming so hot that they jump up with a yell. Here is how you present it.

79

Everyone is now awake. You approach one of the more responsive subjects and ask, "How do you feel?" Once they respond you remark, "You've been under hypnosis quite a while. You need to walk around and get your blood circulating. Have a little walk up and down." The subject will now be stuck to his or her chair. If you want to make doubly sure of this result you can whisper under your breath the word "stuck!" to remind the subject.

He or she will struggle to get out of the chair and not be able to do so. You capitalize on this situation and build up the laughs with it. And of course all this hoopla will remind the other volunteers of what they are supposed to do when it is their turn. You address this by remarking to the other volunteers, "I don't know what is wrong with him. Show him what to do. Stand up and walk around"

Of course, the other subjects will follow your cue (actually not follow it!) and all of them will struggle to get out of their chairs. They will pull, tug and struggle but get nowhere.

Finally, you say, "We will have to use the emergency method. One, two, three, HOT!" The subjects will leap from their chairs as if they had suddenly become hot. The audience will laugh uproariously and you now dismiss your volunteers back into the crowd to a big round of applause from the audience.

At this point you address the audience, "Oh, I just want to check that nobody has left anything on stage. Sometimes people forget things and leave them on stage. Has anyone left anything on stage?" Things start to go a bit crazy here with people searching everywhere for their belly buttons. They might come back up on stage whereupon you tell them that it isn't there and perhaps it is somewhere in the audience. They will perhaps ask people in the audience where the belly button is.

After playing this nonsense up for a while I bring the show to a close with a very dramatic and hilarious finale. You will remember that earlier in the show someone in the audience was accused of stealing a canary. You suddenly point to him or her exclaiming "It's OK. I know who has your belly button. That man (or woman) there has stolen your belly button. Go and ask him for it back!"

They will all descend on your victim and you had better suggest, "You will not physically attack him!" to make sure things don't get out of hand! They will harass him demanding the return of their missing belly buttons and the audience will find this absolutely hilarious! However, before things get too out of hand you suddenly announce, "Back to normal! Your belly buttons are back. Your belly button is back! And all suggestions from tonight are removed. All suggestions from tonight are removed!"

Your participants will all look mightily relieved and will stop harassing the audience member whereupon you proclaim, "Give our volunteers a big round of applause"

And so the show ends. I have just described my own show as a template for you to put together your own performance. It is really only a guideline for you. There are many other skits out there to be found in other hypnosis shows that you might view, plus other stage hypnosis books you might read not to mention skits you would find on the internet. If there is something in my own show already described that you prefer not to use then by all means drop it. If you wish to keep a certain skit in but change it somewhat be my guest. You have the template. Best of luck with it!

The Royal Road to Stage Hypnotism • Mark Lewis

CHAPTER EIGHT
Odds And Ends

The purpose of this chapter is to give you more information and clear up some odds and ends which haven't been mentioned in previous chapters. Chapter Seven gives you the entire show that I have performed for many years. As I previously indicated you can chop and change it around as you see fit. You can add your own routines or remove some of the skits I have described.

This brings me to deal with:

Show Length

The length of a hypnosis show depends on a number of factors including the sort of venue where you are booked to appear. I have seen 45 minute shows up to performances that have lasted 3 hours, albeit with an intermission!

The length of the show described in the previous chapter is around 1 hour and 15 minutes. Sometimes I have lengthened it to 1 hour and 30 minutes by including some magic at the beginning of the performance. In addition to being a stage hypnotist I am also a stage magician which enables me to do this.

However, for most performance venues nowadays such as school and university shows, fairs and exhibitions and corporate events an hour show is about right. There are indeed other venues where longer shows are appropriate such as theatre shows etc;

It is actually quite difficult to present a show in less than one hour although I have seen it done successfully. That is because it takes, in most cases, about 30 minutes to complete the introductory talk, then the waking suggestion tests both in the audience and then on the stage, and finally the hypnotic induction itself. This means that half an hour has transpired before your subjects even get started in taking part in the main activity of the show being the skits themselves.

It is true that some stage hypnotists have found way to cut corners and get to the meat of the show in an a more expedited manner but I don't accede to that school of thought myself. I find the quicker you put people into hypnosis the quicker they come out of it! You build more credibility with the longer procedure I have outlined and not only that, you will find the waking suggestions and other preliminaries very good entertainment in themselves.

As for the induction itself there is a school of thought among certain stage hypnotists that fast inductions are the way to go on the supposition that the longer inductions are slow going and boring to the audience. I don't agree with that notion one bit. I remember the very first time before I even took up hypnotism, I watched a slow induction of the type I have explained in this book and I was fascinated and held spellbound by watching the various participants gradually drift into hypnosis. I believe if the induction is presented properly and with a certain authority it can be the most powerful part of the show.

In fact, although comedy is usually a very important part of a stage hypnosis show I also believe a certain amount of awe and wonder at the phenomena itself is a very good thing too and makes a nice contrast to the hilarity of the show. You can still have a good show without it being a great big bag of laughs and nothing else. Gasps from the audience as well as laughs is a good thing to aim for.

Magic And Hypnosis

I mentioned earlier that I sometimes include magic at the beginning of the show. Of course, I realize that many if not most of the readers of this book will not be magicians but I am sure some will be, so I might as well include this brief section for their consideration.

Odds And Ends

I only do about ten minutes of magic before going on to the hypnosis part of the show. However, I have known and seen performers present a very long performance, usually in a theatre and there is an intermission halfway through the show. I have seen a couple of people present the first half of the show with magic only and after the intermission do another hour or so of hypnotism.

It actually works very well indeed and results in a very well balanced show for the pleasure of the audience.

The reason I personally use magic at the beginning of the show is that in enhances my prestige and makes the actual hypnosis of the subjects easier to achieve. Another thing which helps significantly in encouraging people to come on stage to volunteer is that I do one very powerful card trick on stage where I use a volunteer from the audience. I treat this person with the utmost courtesy during this trick and this encourages people to come on stage later for the hypnotism segment later. They realize that I will treat them with as much courtesy as I did with the person assisting me with the magic.

It is not absolutely essential to use magic in a hypnosis show and in fact most stage hypnotists manage very well without it. However, if you are already a magician and indeed able to incorporate it, you will find that it could be a very good thing. One caveat though; make sure your magic is excellent otherwise it will lower your prestige and do you more harm than good!

Audience Size

The size of the audience has a direct bearing on the success of your show and the way you go about performing it. It is well known among stage hypnotists that the more people in the crowd the better. This is of course because you have a bigger selection of suggestible volunteers to draw from.

Conversely, the less people you have in the audience the harder it gets. There are many stage hypnotists who will refuse to perform if there are less than say, 50 people in the audience. This is because it is much tougher to obtain suggestible subjects.

However, it can still be done if you are very careful and know what you are doing. A lot will depend on the make up of your audience. If you are lucky enough to have a good percentage of the crowd to be young people you can certainly be in with a chance of getting good results since those who are in their late teens or early twenties are the best age group to go into trance which they do very easily indeed. The only exception is a corporate event where young people don't want to make fools of themselves in front of their bosses in case it affects their future career!

On the other hand, if you have an older crowd, especially senior citizens, things will become much more challenging whether you have a small audience or a large one. I would certainly avoid a hypnosis show for senior citizens no matter the size of the audience! The possibility of finding good subjects will be seriously diminished.

Having said that on a few occasions I have been greatly surprised when I have had senior citizens on stage do crazy things. In fact, one or two of them have become so activated and animated I have been a bit worried that they might become over excited and hurt themselves!

I will say that volunteers of a mature age, not necessarily seniors, reacting well to hypnotic suggestions can be more convincing and effective than a bunch of teenagers running around on stage acting like lunatics!

Anyway, back to the size of the audience. If there are less than say 25 to 30 people you are probably better off not doing a hypnosis show in the first place. If I get a call from a potential booker who wants to book a hypnosis show I always ask the size of the audience. If it is on the smaller side I will try to persuade them to have a magic show instead. Of course, you have to be a magician to do this!

Odds And Ends

Sometimes you will get to a venue and the amount of people you were expecting to be there don't show up for some reason and you have to do the best you can. The procedure I recommend if you get caught out this way is to hypnotize the entire audience! Go through the introductory talk and waking suggestion tests earlier outlined and then inform the crowd that you would like to let everyone experience the power of hypnosis and then go through the normal induction. If there are only say, 20 people in the audience, you might just find a tiny few, say 3 to 5 people who seem to be really suggestible. Keep an eye on those few, then wake the rest up using the procedure already outlined but before doing so go to each potential "hot" subject and tap them on the shoulder saying, "those of you who feel my me tap your shoulder will remain in trance while everyone else awakens. Remember you will remain firmly in trance"

After you have done this the rest of the audience will awaken, (not that they were really asleep!) and you will left with a few "live ones". You can now continue with your normal show using your selected subjects. By all means leave them in the audience for the first few tests then direct these people to open their eyes "remaining firmly in trance" and to take their seats in the performing area whereupon you get them to close their eyes again and you continue with the show.

I think this is the best option to pursue if you end up with a smaller audience than you originally expected

Incidentally, this topic reminds me of a point that I forgot to mention. I have occasionally been invited to perform my hypnosis show in private houses. It has never worked well so I advise turning the booking down (or if you are a magician offer that alternative instead). Perhaps my readers will have more success than I have but the odds are against the stage hypnotist for two reasons. The first is the tendency to smaller audiences as I have just outlined. The second is that guests in a private house tend to be reluctant to act too crazy on someone else's property!

Outside Noises

Sometimes when performing there will be outside noises going on during the hypnotic induction. This can be a distraction and detrimental to the trance process. Although as you will have seen in the induction chapter of this book you will have explained to the audience that you need them to be as quiet as possible there will still be occasions when outside noises are going to take place and be out of your control.

For example I have worked at fairs and the noise from the rides were quite a problem. At some venues you might get drunks in the crowd heckling. Perhaps there is a loud unexpected crash when someone drops something. I think the worst thing that ever happened to me during an induction was a very loud fire alarm going off and refusing to stop!

When I first started learning stage hypnosis I practiced at lectures during psychic fairs. In addition to being a hypnotist and magician I am also a palmist and tarot card reader. At these events the psychic readers had the opportunity to give lectures on their specialty. As an exhibitor at these events, I decided that these lecture opportunities would give me a good way of practicing stage hypnosis.

The snag was that there was often a lot of noise outside the lecture area where many times the only separation from the main event was a mere curtained area. I always had a bit of trouble dealing with the racket from outside especially during the induction process.

Fortunately there was an exhibitor there who happened to be a hypnotherapist promoting his services. He had told me that at one time he had been a stage hypnotist before he turned to hypnotherapy. He saw my show a few times and could see that I was having difficulty with the surrounding noise problem so he took me aside and gave me the advice that I am going to give you now.

He told me the best way to fight the noise issue was not to fight it since I wouldn't win the fight anyway! Instead, he ad-

Odds And Ends

vised me that the best thing to do is to say to the subjects, "Any outside noises will not disturb you. Any outside noises will put you further and further and deeper and deeper into hypnosis".

That was all I had to do and it worked like a charm! The only time that it only half worked was the time I mentioned when the very, very loud fire alarm went off and wouldn't stop! However, even then I got some kind of result. They would open their eyes and I just told them to go back down into trance again. I had to keep doing this a few times along with the suggestion that the noise would put them into trance.

Of course, along with the noise they may also have been worrying if a fire was going to engulf them while they had their eyes closed! Fortunately, it was a false alarm and even more fortunately it has never happened again!

Posters

I have found a very useful aid to obtaining good hypnotic subjects is the use of posters proclaiming your appearance at the venue. It is well known that prestige and expectation is a very powerful aid to a stage hypnotism show. By that I mean the prestige of the performer and the expectation that a hypnotism show is going to take place.

I will deal with the prestige issue first. The stronger the prestige of the hypnotist the more likely the show is going to be a success. You will remember that I mentioned in an earlier chapter that you should never let the audience know you are a beginner. The more they think you are an expert the more likely they are to go into trance. The bigger your reputation the better the results you will get. Word of mouth of how amazing you are will draw people to your show and your prestige will win the day. The stronger your prestige is the stronger the show will be. Posters or in fact any kind of advertising will help you to build that prestige. Very often the person who books you will have their own way of promoting your services and of course this will help the prestige factor. However, you can't always rely on this so I suggest that you help them out by having nicely designed posters advertising your event.

I normally, depending on the venue, will send about half a dozen posters to the organizer of the event to distribute them where they see fit. If it is an event where I have control over the matter then I put the posters up myself.

Now let me try to explain the expectation factor. The very worst thing that can happen to a stage hypnotist is if he is booked as "surprise" entertainment. This situation can be an invitation to disaster. It is essential that the audience should know in advance what kind of show they are about to see. If a hypnotist is sprung on them unexpectedly there will be great reluctance to volunteer and the few that do will not go into trance very well.

Conversely if they know well in advance they are going to witness a stage hypnotism show it will build up the anticipation and excitement resulting in them being eager to participate and be half hypnotized before they even arrive at the show!

Again, this is where the posters will be extremely helpful. I highly recommend that this is something you give consideration to. The photograph will give you some idea of what I am talking about.

Assistants

The use of an assistant or even multiple assistants is often seen in a stage hypnosis show. Some performers utilize them and some don't. There are advantages and disadvantages to them. I can think of only two disadvantages as I write this but there may possibly be more that I haven't thought of.

One disadvantage is that if you get the wrong ones, it can do more harm than good! I have had some very good assistants over the years but alas I still remember one fellow who was a little too extrovert for my taste. You would think he was doing the show instead of me! He made inappropriate comments in front of the event organizer which embarrassed me. He started showing magic tricks to people before the show when I wanted him to stay in the background and generally speaking, he was a hindrance rather than a help.

The other obvious disadvantage of an assistant is that you have to pay him or her! Unless of course you happen to be married to your assistant!

Now for the advantages. Or perhaps I should describe the advantages for me personally since one size does not fit all. What is an advantage for me may not necessarily be an advantage for you. I expect my first couple of examples will apply to me rather than to you.

First I am one of those strange people on this planet who has no idea how to drive and is in no position to learn for reasons I don't wish to get into. Besides it will give the nosier of my readers something to wonder about. Anyway, this one reason I use an assistant for should be obvious. He or she will, unlike myself be a normal human who does have the ability to drive.

Another advantage which applies to me personally may perhaps also be somewhat more applicable to a few other of my readers so perhaps it will be useful information for them too.

By nature I am a shy and not a particularly sociable person. I don't feel comfortable around people I do not know and that applies particularly to people I have to meet and deal with at the venue such as the MC, stage staff, sound operators and of course the person who booked me to appear. Oddly enough I suffer from stage fright in reverse! I can't wait to get on stage to get away from all the people off stage! The stage is my second home so I don't get nervous there. My nervousness occurs when I am offstage rather than onstage!

I know that it may seem odd that I am far more at ease with a large crowd of several hundred people than I am just talking to one single solitary person that I don't know! Still, I will let the psychologists among you figure it out. I haven't got time to do so since I am supposed to be writing a book! Anyway, hav-

Odds And Ends

ing someone with me eases the discomfort of dealing with strangers.

Now let me go on to some other advantages which will no doubt be more applicable to most of my readers. One major advantage is that it adds to the, for want of a better phrase, "production value". In other words, it fills the stage better and makes you appear to be more important than you actually are!

Incidentally although some stage hypnotists use several assistants, I personally find it to be overkill and they tend to get in the way and the show looks a bit messy. Besides you have to pay more people! I only use one assistant and find that more than enough.

An assistant can be very useful from a safety point of view. This may well be the biggest advantage of them all. Things can go a little crazy on stage and you have to be on guard constantly to make sure people don't hurt themselves. I have reason to believe that broken necks on stage are not a terribly good addition to the performance! An alert and capable assistant can help you tremendously here and step in to help if things are getting out of hand.

Incidentally with regard to this particular point, generally speaking younger volunteers tend to go a little crazier than people of more mature age. High school and university shows can result in some very animated behavior which is not necessarily as safe as it should be. An assistant is particularly helpful in these circumstances as an extra pair of eyes to watch out for things getting out of control and to step in when necessary.

Your assistant can also help you spot fakers among your subjects who might start to make faces or act stupidly when your back is turned. An assistant makes it more difficult for them to do this without being discovered. After all, four eyes are better than two! Incidentally, if you happen to hear some unexpected laughter from the audience that might be a sign that someone on stage is faking the trance, making signs or faces to the audience when your back is turned, but when you turn around again, they go back into an assumed trance so you are none the wiser.

Things can go a little crazy on stage with people running about and chairs shifting position all over the place. An assistant can be of great help in controlling the chaos and putting chairs back where they are supposed to be. They can also hand you various props at various times. They can introduce you on stage. They can sometimes quietly give you some suggestions about certain things that might be happening on stage that you miss. One of the most useful functions of an assistant is that you have someone to discuss certain aspects of the show after the performance on the way home.

I have often worked without one and it has worked out very well so it is not 100 percent necessary. However, there is no denying that providing you can find the right person it can help the show substantially and be well worth it.

Stooges

When I first started to study stage hypnosis, I was naturally very concerned about what might happen if I had a whole bunch of participants on stage and found I wasn't able to hypnotize a single one of them. A scary proposition to be sure!

I therefore decided that it might be a good idea to hire a couple of people to come on stage and act as secret assistants and pretend to go into "trance" and carry out the suggestions required. I did try this route a few times until I realized that the genuine subjects reacted far better than the fake ones! Besides the fakes were often bad actors and they often did more harm than good because of this.

I finally asked a renowned stage hypnotist if I should use stooges for my first few shows to make sure I didn't end up with a whole bunch of people on stage that wouldn't cooperate and simply refuse to go into trance. He scoffed at me saying, "If you use stooges you are dead!" I decided to take his advice and not bother with stooges any more. Mind you I heard later that

Odds And Ends

this particular hypnotist used stooges himself! I guess not everyone practices what they preach!

However, there is a way of getting subjects to cooperate without having to turn them into fully fledged stooges. You will notice that on several occasions in my description of the show in the previous chapter I have secretly cued the volunteers under my breath to do certain things on stage to enhance the proceedings.

There is also something known in the business as "contract players". I have already referred to them in the very first chapter of this book. They are not hypnotized and you know they are not hypnotized but they are happy to help you out and assist you in putting on a good show. These people can be very useful indeed providing they are good actors. They are stooges that are not really stooges because you have not made any arrangement with them to play along. You just take advantage of the situation!

I would now like to describe an emergency method that has gotten me out of trouble on a few occasions when I have had a group of people on stage and for one reason or another haven't been able to hypnotize any of them. Some stage hypnotists have told me that they disapprove of this method probably because they think it isn't really genuine hypnosis. However, I feel that if I have to choose between looking like an incompetent idiot on stage for an hour or more or doing things "incorrectly" and getting good and sometimes great results from it I shall most certainly go for the "incorrect" method!

Here it is. Let us assume that for some reason you just can't get anyone to go "under". Actually, this seems a good point to mention that alcohol is often the cause of subpar shows. It is possible that in some circumstances you may get some inebriated volunteers on stage. A little alcohol can actually help in getting your subjects going. Alas too much of it hinders. With this in mind don't go on too late at night if alcohol is being served. That is an invitation to disaster. Tell the booker that if the audience gets too well-oiled it will spoil the show and the money they are paying you will be wasted.

I am happy to tell you what I do not only if the volunteers are drunk but also when they are recalcitrant. As I have already mentioned this method will not please some stage hypnotists but I have to live in the real world. I have been booked to entertain by whatever means possible and I have found this is the best means possible. Sure, you can storm off the stage and refuse to perform but that is the way to at best produce bad feelings and at worst difficulty in getting paid.

I am sure as hell not going to stand up there for an hour struggling because of misplaced misgivings some stage hypnotists will have concerning my system. This is only used in emergencies and has got me out of trouble on quite a few occasions.

If I see that I am getting nowhere I then wake them all up and say something along the lines that there is something known as pyramiding hypnosis which means that hypnosis is easier to achieve when it is attempted a second time. I then give each person a card with wavy lines on and tell them to stare at it then I go into the induction. Miraculously this will get terrific subjects out of nowhere whereas moments before the subjects were pretty useless.

Now this is the bit the purists won't like. A few of those cards do not have wavy lines at all. Instead, they have a message telling your subjects to play along with it. They always do. That way you save the show.

Now I realize there are disadvantages to this system. Stooges talk. But by then you will be well away from the venue with the money in your pocket. It isn't perfect but it is far better than standing there on stage looking foolish for an hour. No thanks.

And oddly enough a strange thing happens when you ask people to be an instant stooge in this way. They often relax and go into REAL hypnosis however you define it! Many, many times I have done this and have been astonished that the subjects cannot remember having been given the cards even when I speak to them privately about it! No kidding. Really.

I still remember performing for a police association event and I had to use this method. At first I found it difficult to hypnotize anyone so I gave the "stooge" cards to a few subjects and the show went over sensationally well. A year later I was booked to do the show again at the same event. Just before the show started a man approached me and I immediately recognized him from the year before as one of the "instant stooges" I had give the card to. He surprised me by telling me that he couldn't believe how he had done all the crazy things the year before and he didn't remember doing them. His friends showed him photographs of his antics to prove he really did them. Up to that point he didn't believe their tales of his mayhem and madness!

I realized that he had completely forgotten that I had given him the card with the secret message to play along and had actually gone into "hypnosis" however you define it. This wasn't the only time this phenomenon happened either. I have at other times come into contact with people who remembered being hypnotized but seemed to have no notion or recollection whatsoever of the secret instructions that were given to them.

I suppose I should give you the secret wording on the "stooge cards". It says, "We are going to have some laughs and fool the audience. When I ask you to do some funny things please do as I secretly tell you. Thanks"

Sometimes you can get similar results without the cards by secretly cueing people as I already mentioned. I did hear of one hypnotist who once he secured his volunteers on stage and before he commenced his induction would secretly whisper to them "Just pretend". That was all he needed to say!

I do remember one occasion when I was booked to perform for a corporate party. One of the volunteers on stage was the boss of the company. He was a bit skeptical and even slightly belligerent and refused to co-operate. His lack of co-operation influenced the rest of them not to co-operate too. I was tempted to use the card technique that I described earlier but instead whispered to him, "just play along for the sake of the show" None of the other participants heard me. And from that moment on he was as good as gold doing all sorts of stupid things with great enthusiasm. But here is the funny thing. His subordinates on stage, as soon as they saw the boss was following instructions and making a fool of himself, decided from that moment on that it was all right for them to appear as daft as the boss was. It was a terrific show and one of the best I ever did!

Music And Sound Effects

I am no expert on this subject so I won't talk about it much except to say that if you can incorporate some music and sound effects into your show it will enhance the show and production value significantly. I particularly recommend using suitable tranquil music for the induction process as well as music to introduce you to the audience when you first come on stage. With regard to sound effects, I have used recordings of birds, ocean waves, thunderstorms in my Hawaii sequence described earlier in this book.

CHAPTER NINE
Hypnosis Audio Transcription

When I was writing this book I came across an old cassette tape that I once made explaining how to go about becoming a stage hypnotist. It occurred to me that it might well be a fitting chapter for this book. I suspect it might duplicate some of the information I have already written although I don't know if it does since I haven't listened to it in years. Anyway, here it is for what it is worth!

Transcript

Hello. My name is Mark Lewis. I am a professional stage hypnotist and magician. On this tape I am going to explain to the best of my ability how to become a stage hypnotist. Actually, this tape can only give you a general guide on how to do it. Sooner or later you are actually going to have to go out and try it for the first time. Now that's a scary thought. I think that's probably why you don't see too many stage hypnotists, at least not as many hypnotists as you see magicians. That is probably because a magician has his act under his own control. He can rehearse in private and not go on stage until he knows the trick will work. If he does find that the trick does not go over well he can work on it further-or eliminate it if necessary. A hypnotist can't do this. A hypnotic show generally lasts a long time, generally an hour or 90 minutes. Some hypnotists even do a couple of hours or more. So it's a pretty daunting task for a neophyte hypnotist to go out on stage for the first time and perform for an hour or more not knowing if the hypnosis will work or not. How is he going to do an hour show without finding live subjects to practice on? And even if by some miracle he actually found volunteers to rehearse with, how is he going to guarantee that the new people that come up on stage when he performs for real will do the same thing that the rehearsal volunteers will do?

A magician can take a new trick, rehearse and practice it to the best of his ability then put it in his show buffeting it in between material that he knows well. For example, he can put a strong trick that he knows well before the new item and follow the new item by another tried and tested effect. A sandwich technique. I call it a new trick sandwich. If the new trick goes well, great! If it fails some of the other old reliable stuff will take the pressure off. A hypnotist can't do this so what does the new hypnotist do? When I first started I got some good advice from a legendary old time stage hypnotist. He basically told me to rehearse to the tables and chairs at home. Yes, that's it! Talk to the furniture! "GET YOUR PATTER RIGHT" he said. Actually, what he said was "Get your patter right and then just go out and do it" Have the chutzpah to go out and do it. I shall explain "chutzpah" later on. Anyway, get your patter right and then just go out and do it. It is very important. Rehearse, rehearse and rehearse until you are sick of it. Imagine in your mind that the subjects are up on stage doing what you want them to do. The fact that they might not do it in actual performance you have to put out of your mind for the moment. Assume that they will do what you want them to do and rehearse that routine just like you would rehearse a magic show. The only difference is that you are rehearsing with invisible props and your props are human beings. When you first start get that routine in your head and do not deviate from it until you get performing experience behind you. Anyway, after many hours rehearsing this embryonic act you will have to go out and try it out before a live audience. And when I say many hours I mean MANY hours. Now it doesn't have to be complete drudgery. I did about an hour a day for three months before I dared to go out before a live audience.

Anyway, this is where chutzpah comes in. You cannot do a hypnotism show without chutzpah. Let me define it. Chutzpah is an old Yiddish word meaning nerve. Or to put it crudely something that jugglers use in their act. Chutzpah is best defined as a man murdering his parents and asking the court for leniency on the grounds that he is an orphan.

Anyway, sooner or later you are going to have to develop the Chutzpah to go out on stage and do this untried and untested act. But remember that it is not completely untested. You have spent hours on it at home-remember?

Your first show will be an eerie experience. When you first get people doing crazy things on stage you will get such a strange happy feeling going through you that it is hard to describe. Now you may say, "What happens if nothing works?" Well, then of course you've got problems. Now I was lucky. I had an opportunity to practice with live audiences on a regular basis at psychic fairs. In a former life I was a professional psychic consultant. I was actually very successful at it. For a few years I worked at psychic fairs all across Canada. At these fairs the various psychics were offered lecture time. They didn't get paid for this but it enabled them to promote their skills to the visitors to the fair and it would encourage them to come to the psychic's booth to have a paid reading. For a while I did psychometry demonstrations and I found that this got me business at my booth. However, after a while I realized that this would be a good place to practice stage hypnotism. The audiences were small, only 20 to 30 people usually, and there were outside noises and distractions from the fair itself. And only half an hour was available for lecture time. So, in some ways it was not ideal but the opportunities to practice were still great nevertheless. I did notice a falling off of visitors coming to my booth after the hypnotism show for some reason, probably because it was a carnival type entertainment rather than a serious discussion of psychic divination. Nevertheless. It was still worthwhile because it did give me the chance to practice. The missing revenue has been well made up for because of the many thousands of dollars since because of my paid hypnotism shows before the public.

Incidentally a stage hypnotist can earn fees that a magician can only dream of. I just thought I'd mention it.

Anyway, my first show at the psychic fairs was a great success, people were hypnotized and I was more amazed than the audience was. Of course, the audience was amazed too and I became a bit of a sensation at the psychic fair. Unfortunately, however this didn't last because my second, third and fourth show was an unmitigated disaster. Nobody gave the appearance of being vaguely under hypnosis. So all I got out of those shows was embarrassment.

The fifth show I did was mildly successful but nowhere as good as the first show I had performed. The sixth, seventh and eighth shows were disasters. In fact, so were the ninth and tenth! In fact it got so bad that I asked a friend of mine who helped me out at psychic fairs, "Why don't you go on the stage and be a stooge for me?" He refused on the grounds that he didn't wish to be part of a sinking ship!

Anyway, eventually the show improved over time and nowadays I earn ten times what I would get doing magic at a kid's birthday party! However, I don't believe I would have stuck it out if the first show hadn't been good. So your first successful show is all important. It will give you the confidence to carry on. The message is chutzpah. You need to go out and die the death on stage. Another thing you definitely need is persistence. Keep trying no matter how many times you die a death, no matter how many times you fail to hypnotize people. Eventually the magic day will come when you have a stage full of volunteers doing all sorts of crazy things and all the practice, rehearsal and suffering embarrassment at non existent hypnotism will fade into insignificance as you bask in the astonishment and adulation of the audience.

With regard to this persistence I have been talking about here is a little story. There is a terrific stage hypnotist I once knew in Ireland. One of the best I have ever seen. However, I did hear from various gossiping magician sources that in the beginning he found it as tough as I did when he first started. Apparently it didn't work a lot of the time when he did it and in the end he hired a bar room and he performed every night for practice until he got the hang of it. Even then I heard that he found it rough going. Sometimes it would work and sometimes it didn't. The story that I heard is that it wasn't until he got a booking on a cruise ship that he got consistently successful results.

Now after all this time he has been a successful performer for many, many years but in the beginning he found it tough. I am telling you this story so you realize the value of persistence. Do not give up too quickly. Of course, you may be one of the lucky ones and get good results straight away on a consistent basis. Well, if that's the case thank your lucky stars.

One way to reduce the odds of failing when you first start is to have a stooge or two in the show. That way if the worst happens you have your own people to fall back on. This might be a good way to give you confidence in the beginning but I would advise you to get rid of the stooges as soon as you can. Once you start to get genuine subjects on a consistent basis you won't need the stooges any more. You will find that audiences can often spot stooges a mile away, generally speaking. And after a while you will soon see that the genuine subjects will far outperform the stooges anyway! Still, if it makes you feel better when you first start I won't argue with you.

Although you can learn from your mistakes it is usually a better idea to learn from other people's mistakes. So you might as well learn from mine!

The standard wisdom in some books on stage hypnotism is that you should get lots of experience hypnotizing people in one to one situations before attempting to try it out on stage. I read once that you should hypnotize several dozen people over a few years before trying it out on stage. I did not find this approach worked for me. First of all, I found it difficult to find eager guinea pigs, second of all even when I did find someone they wouldn't go under hypnosis anyway!

Actually, you will find that it is ten times easier to hypnotize people in a stage situation than it is one to one. The stage is a foreign environment for people not in show business or any occupation where they have to stand up in public. Consequently, when people come up to volunteer on stage they can be a little disorientated –the lights, the music, the curtains, the tension from being on stage and above all the expectancy centred on each subject by the audience. Call it social expectation----the desire not to be a party pooper—to please the audience and also to please the hypnotist.

All this plays a part in making it easier to hypnotize people on stage. There is also the dynamics of the group situation. If one person in the group goes along with the situation so will the others. When I used to make a living demonstrating and selling magic tricks to crowds in fairs, exhibitions and department stores I knew that if one person was persuaded to buy something it would encourage other people in the crowd to do the same. The same psychology applies in stage hypnosis. People are like sheep. If one person does something the others will follow. Also, on stage it is easier to follow the directions of the hypnotist rather than striking out on your own.

Another thing to consider is the numbers factor. The odds are in your favour simply because out of an audience of say, 200 people you are bound to find around 15 of them who are prone to being suggestible enough to be your best subjects. The reason I found it difficult at psychic fairs was partly because I had such small audiences and I would be lucky to find enough people to be good subjects.

Anyway, it is far, far easier to hypnotize people on stage that it is one to one so although it may be useful to get some practice in by hypnotizing people in a one-to-one situation I do not actually think it is strictly necessary despite what some books say. I think the most important thing to rehearse thoroughly is to get your patter right. Then take a chance and get out and do it, using a stooge if you must to give you confidence. Do your first show for free if necessary. Or in any event charge a low fee. It is most important to get performing experience at any cost. Don't worry about money in the early stages. Learn how to do it properly first. The money will come later.

I met a young hypnotist once. He was just starting and his first shows were pitiful. Let's be honest—they weren't very good. And he also had the added disadvantage of busybody magicians in the audience criticizing his work. I mean, yet they would never have the nerve in a million years to get the sheer courage to get out and do it. Now this young fellow is earning ten times the money his critics are—not that they did many shows anyway.

Most magicians are very good at criticizing and the worst critics are the amateurs who don't have the guts to perform before the public. I was once told by a wise old veteran performer "Audacity and bluff -that is the sign of a good entertainer". This is especially true of a stage hypnotist. You have to have the guts to go out and die a death a few times until you get the hang of it. If you find this prospect unappetizing the compensation is that once you get the hang of it your income will quadruple. I know mine has. But there is no gain without the pain. If it were too easy there would be a million stage hypnotists out there and the money would go down. I don't know where you are going to find your first audiences---that is up to you. Not everyone is going to be able to do psychic fairs so I shall have to let you figure that one out. Probably your best bet is to already be a professional magician, then you will probably find the audiences to try it on faster than the amateur. Actually, you should probably not attempt stage hypnotism unless you already have experience as a performer of some sort, whether it is as a mentalist, a magician or even some other branch of the entertainment business. I do remember one prominent stage hypnotist who originally started as a former radio host and disc jockey, for example.

Stage hypnotism is not for the faint of heart. You also have to be a showman, a good talker—used to dealing with people on stage. In fact, the stage should be your second home. So, in actual practice I don't think you have a lot of chance of success in this field unless you are used to working before the public. I will give you a little proof of this. Although there have been many, many hypnotherapists who originally came from the ranks of stage entertainers there have been very few, if any, hypnotherapists who have gravitated to the stage. In other words, it worked one way but not the other. To be an entertainer is vastly different from being a clinical hypnotist or a psychologist. Your job as a stage hypnotist will be vastly easier providing you are a showman by nature.

Now you might find things a little easier if you know what hypnotism actually is. What makes people do these crazy things on stage. Actually, I am not 100 percent sure myself! So perhaps I am going to be of limited help here. I do know there is quite a bit of debate among psychologists as to what the hypnotic state actually is. The debaters are divided into two camps. The state theorists and the non-state theorists. Simply put, the non-state theorists believe there is no such thing as the hypnotic state—and the state theorists believe there is such a thing.

I don't have time to debate the matter here. Suffice it to say that I tend to be a non-state theorist. In other words, I don't believe I have ever hypnotized anybody! I do believe some of my subjects have deluded themselves into a belief that I have hypnotized them but that is another matter! Maybe that belief in itself constitutes hypnosis and the whole thing is a matter of semantics. One man's hypnosis is another man's load of nonsense! Now having said this I am not entirely sure that I am right. After doing this thousands of times I have seen some very strange behaviour that is certainly not acting so although I tend to be a non-state theorist I am not entirely sure of what's going on. Maybe they ARE hypnotized—I don't really know. I am tempted to say I don't really care as long as people act like they are hypnotized and do crazy things on stage. But on the other hand, I think you will be a better hypnotist if you form some opinion about it.

Most books on the subject are written by state theorists. The best book supporting the skeptical point of view is titled "They Call It Hypnosis" by Robert Baker published by Prometheus Books. A very famous performer by the unusual moniker "The Amazing Kreskin" is quoted extensively in the book and of course he is a leading non-state theorist.

Actually, you will find that many people will follow your suggestions for different reasons. One person on stage may have deluded himself that he is hypnotized and genuinely believes that he is. Another person may be simulating it. Another may be doing it because of social expectation. Still another may be doing it because he or she is showing off.

Actually, I don't mind if somebody is simulating hypnosis on stage if they are good at the simulation. In other words, I don't mind them acting if they are good actors and they don't try to spoil the show. By the way you can find out if someone is genuinely under hypnosis by lifting their arm. If it is limp they are under hypnosis—if the arm is tense you know they are acting. One thing you need to be on the alert for are subjects who are pretending to be hypnotized and as soon as your back is turned they start laughing or making faces at the audience. When you turn round they go back to sleep and act as if nothing has happened. You can identify these jokers if you have an assistant in the act who can let you know who the troublemaker is. Or you can have a friend in the audience who signals to you by holding up a number of fingers to indicate which chair the offender is sitting on. You should be especially alert to unexpected laughter when your back is turned.

Anyway, a lot of your work is actually done before the show starts. The key to hypnotizing people on stage is expectation and anticipation. I think those are most important words in stage hypnosis. Expectation and anticipation. If a volunteer expects to be hypnotized he or she probably will be. I always send posters to the venue a few weeks before the show. I ask the organizers to put up the posters or at the very least to inform everyone that a hypnotist is going to be appearing. This gives the audience time to "hype" themselves up and they will be half hypnotized before the show even starts.

On no account should the entertainment be booked as a "surprise". This is asking for trouble since the audience will not have had time to get themselves mentally prepared for the show. As a result, the hypnotic results may be a little "iffy". That is if you can even get volunteers in the first place. By the way, you can almost tell at the very beginning how well your show is going to go over when you ask for volunteers. If they reluctantly come up in dribs and drab you have a tough show on your hands. You will have to pull out all the stops. This is where the men will be separated from the boys. Where the bad hypnotists are separated from the good. You will need every ounce of showmanship and good hypnotic techniques to pull it off. Conversely, if you get more people up on stage than you can handle, if there is an eager rush of volunteers, a ton of eager beavers shall we say, then you are going to have a great show!

Another thing. On no account should the audience know you are a beginner. If they think you are just starting they will not go into the trance state. The prestige of the hypnotist is very important. If they assume you are an expert they will go into trance. This is another reason you must rehearse your patter thoroughly. The audience must believe you have done this a thousand times. If your patter sounds slick and smooth it will help to convince the volunteers you are a professional.

Now a word or two about problem audiences. First of all, an audience of seniors could spell trouble. Generally, the younger the crowd the more successful you will be. When I say young I mean high school age and up. I do not believe in getting kids up on stage and hypnotizing them. I will send people back if they are 14 years old or under. I am not overly keen on 15 year olds either. It lowers the importance of the show and also makes me look irresponsible to the parents. The ideal age for good hypnotic subjects is 18 years to late 20s. This is why high school, college and university shows are very effective and easy to do. Anyway, the older the group the more reserved and dignified they will be. Mind you, I have had some amazing successes. I have found with an audience composed of predominately young people if a senior does volunteer they will often outclass the young people in the crazy things they will do and they often become the stars of the show! However, generally speaking seniors are not good subjects. I think the way around this is either to avoid shows for seniors or make the routines gentle and not too crazy. After all, you don't want them breaking their necks! So limit the amount of action and running around.

Now let's go to the other extreme. It is very rare but you might actually be asked to do a show for kids. And I mean young kids. If you are a magician you could possibly suggest they book your magic instead but of course you can't charge the same as you can for a hypnotism show. I was once talked into doing a hypnotism show for kids. I told the booker that I would only get adults up to help so they organized about 20 young adults to come on stage and the show went quite well. My biggest problem was getting the kids to be quiet during the hypnotic induction. I got away with it because I am an experienced children's entertainer and I managed to get the kids quiet enough to enjoy the show.

At this point let me talk a little about safety on stage. Many stage hypnotists have been sued at some time or other for having hurt the volunteer or supposedly causing them mental damage. Hypnotism can be dangerous to the volunteer on stage if the showman doesn't know what he is doing—or even sometimes if he does! This one of the main reasons that there is so much criticism about stage hypnotism from the medical profession and the hypnotherapy profession. In some jurisdictions stage hypnotism is banned even though the ban is may not be necessarily enforced rigidly. In Britain a few years ago there was a massive uproar in the newspapers about how dangerous stage hypnotism was. There were questions raised in parliament and this commotion went on for quite a few weeks. As a result of the commotion stage hypnotists found business quite slow for a while. I heard that cruise ships operating out of Britain wouldn't touch hypnotism with a long foot pole.

Anyway, you have to take care of this in your patter when inviting people on stage warning that you wish to discourage certain types of people from coming up such as epileptics, etc; especially psychiatric patients. Discourage them from coming up and if you do discover someone on stage that you suspect to be a bit flaky send them back to the audience no matter how good a subject they may appear to be. Be very careful of the physical wellbeing of your volunteers. Check the stage before the show for unexpected hazards. Watch for splinters on the floor, keep an eye out for heavy objects that might topple over and hurt people. Watch out for slippery parts of the stage, for example, water spills. It is a good idea to have a rug placed on stage. Don't have people falling out of their chairs on to a dirty stage. Make sure the volunteers don't attack each other when they get too excited or confrontational! Make sure they don't stamp on each other's hands. Or crash chairs into themselves or each other.

Another thing is that I do not approve of are X-rated or pornographic shows. There are plenty of hypnotists who make their shows an exercise in crudity. I don't think this pays in the long run. It is very bad for the image of stage hypnosis and gives critics further ammunition. I am an old fuddy duddy but I do believe keeping a high tone to my work has paid off. You can be funny without being lewd and disgusting. Enough said.

....

At this point the tape describes a lot of information which has already been described in previous pages of this book that I really am not inclined to repeat again so what I will do to save space is to post further relevant extracts from the tapes in the next chapter.

CHAPTER TEN
More Extracts From The Audiotape

Transcript Excerpts

"I invite a committee on the stage. Now I always have a minimum of ten chairs on the stage. More if I have a large stage and a large audience. If there are too many people on stage, in other words more people than there are chairs I ask the surplus people to stand behind the chairs. It is actually quite possible to hypnotize people standing up so the people behind the chairs are not a problem. That is, providing they rest their hands on the chair in front of them. I also give them the suggestion that their legs are made of steel and they will not fall over."

"Sometimes some judicious whispering to the difficult subjects to the effect of 'put on a good show for the sake of the audience' or perhaps, 'help me out here. We are having difficulty putting people under'. Sometimes that can bring them round but not always. Sometimes this whispering technique works brilliantly with good subjects! You can give them whispered suggestions that the audience do not hear and they will do some really crazy things or say something extremely funny. The audience does not realize that you have secretly primed the volunteers and it looks like the hypnotic state is doubly effective. The volunteers would still follow the suggestions if they were said out loud and it would still be good entertainment. But it is of course much more effective if it is done secretly."

"I then do a couple of waking suggestion stunts on stage. If I have too many people on stage and I want to thin the crowd down I eliminate a few people on the basis of these tests. Actually, even if the volunteers fail on these tests, they will still often make good subjects. I just use the tests as good showmanship and of course it primes and trains the volunteers to follow instructions. This will be useful later on when you actually hypnotize them. In any event the tests make good entertainment in themselves although I may eliminate them if the audience is inebriated or restless."

"Just before I commence the hypnotic induction, I give a little speech to the participants explaining that I am now about to hypnotize them and that it is a safe and pleasant procedure. I explain that this will be useful to them in the future if they wish to give up smoking, suffer from stammering, phobias, or weight control problems. I explain that they will not be unconscious and they will be aware of what is going on around them. I explain to them that any time they want, they can come out of trance simply by opening their eyes."

"I do not subscribe to the trend nowadays towards instant inductions. There are methods of putting the volunteers under very quickly indeed—in fact sometimes in less than 30 seconds. Although the trend today in modern entertainment is to get on with the show and keep the pace of the act going fairly briskly, I do not think these fast inductions methods look very convincing.

Very often the depth of the hypnotic trance is very shallow and the volunteers come out of it very quickly. Even if they do remain hypnotized I think the audience is a bit skeptical. I prefer a slower dramatic induction and the audience becomes fascinated seeing the volunteers gradually drifting off to sleep.

Some hypnotists dull the stage lighting while the induction is taking place. In certain ways this can help induce the hypnotic state and encourage the volunteers to go into trance. It also helps to hide the unwelcome smirks and giggles that some resistant subjects occasionally exhibit. However, the disadvantage of low lighting is that the audience is deprived of seeing the volunteers gradually drifting off into trance. In some ways the hypnotic induction is my favourite part of the show. Even rowdy audiences go quiet as they see the subjects going down deeper and deeper. Some hypnotists and know all amateur magicians find hypnotic inductions boring. I can assure them that audiences do not. They LIKE moderately long inductions!

Now I did say moderately long. I don't think 20-minute inductions, for example---and I have seen this------are a good fit. I don't think an induction should be longer than 10 minutes—and even that may be a little long. Some hypnotists pride themselves on their incredibly short inductions. You know that I don't go along with that. I don't think an induction should be less than 4 minutes long if you want to convince the audience the phenomena is genuine. Too long can be boring but too short does not look real. Anyway, that's my opinion and I am sticking to it."

CHAPTER ELEVEN
Last Word

OK. I guess that's it! I have just described the show I have been doing for years. Of course, the skits I have explained are the ones I use personally and I have found them very effective indeed. However, there is no law saying you have to use any of them if they don't suit you. By all means if you find other skits that you prefer then of course you can substitute them for any of the material I have described. In fact, there are tons and tons of different routines and skits you can use. I have not described them because I have no experience with them.

However, you can discover them for yourself by watching other stage hypnotists when you get the chance. No doubt you will read other books on stage hypnosis in addition to this one and I have no doubt you will find sundry skits therein. Of course there are also many skits to be found on the internet.

I thank you for reading this to the end and I wish you great success in your future stage hypnosis career!

www.ingramcontent.com/pod-product-compliance
Lightning Source LLC
Chambersburg PA
CBHW070336230426
43663CB00011B/2337